Making Sense of Academic Conferences

Based on practical experiences and empirical research, *Making Sense of Academic Conferences* offers an introduction to the world of academic conferences. This accessible text also includes material to support researchers who are organising conferences.

Offering guidance about presenting at, participating in, and planning a conference, it uncovers the purpose of conferences; their role in supporting researcher development; steps involved in selecting and travelling to a conference; routine practices and terminology; strategies for making the most out of conferences. Suitable for doctoral students and early career researchers, this book engages with all aspects of academic conferences, recognising that attending conferences is as much about presenting papers as discos and not spilling your tea on the keynote speaker.

The book is ideally suited for graduate researchers and early career researchers, particularly those who may be going to their first conference, or travelling to their first international conference, and for more experienced academics who are working with novice conference attendees.

James Burford is Assistant Professor of Global Education and International Development in the Department of Education Studies at the University of Warwick, UK.

Emily F. Henderson is Reader in Gender and International Higher Education in the Department of Education Studies at the University of Warwick, UK.

Insider Guides to Success in Academia

Series Editors:
Helen Kara,
Independent Researcher, UK and
Pat Thomson,
The University of Nottingham, UK

The *Insiders' Guides to Success in Academia* address topics too small for a full-length book on their own, but too big to cover in a single chapter or article. These topics have often been the stuff of discussions on social media, or of questions in our workshops. We designed this series to answer these questions in to provide practical support for doctoral and early career researchers. It is geared to concerns that many people experience. Readers will find these books to be companions who provide advice and help to make sense of everyday life in the contemporary university.

We have *therefore*:

- invited scholars with deep and specific expertise to write. Our writers use their research and professional experience to provide well-grounded strategies to particular situations.
- asked writers to collaborate. Most of the books are produced by writers who live in different countries, or work in different disciplines, or both. While it is difficult for any book to cover all the diverse contexts in which potential readers live and work, the different perspectives and contexts of writers goes some way to address this problem.

We understand that the use of the term 'academia' might be read as meaning the university, but we take a broader view. *Pat* does indeed work in a university, but spent a long time working outside of one. Helen is an independent researcher and sometimes works with universities. Both of us understand academic – or scholarly – work as now being conducted in a range of sites, from museums and the public sector to industry research and development laboratories. Academic work is also often undertaken by networks which bring together scholars in various locations. All of our writers understand that this is the case, and use the term 'academic' in this wider sense.

These books are *pocket* sized so that they can be carried around and visited again and again. Most of the books have a mix of examples, stories and exercises as well as explanation and advice. They are written in a collegial tone, and from a position of care as well as knowledge.

Together with *our* writers, we hope that each book in the series can make a positive contribution to the work and life of readers, so that you too can become insiders in scholarship.

Helen Kara, PhD *FAcSS*,
independent *researcher*
https://helenkara.com/
@DrHelenKara (Twitter/Insta)

Pat Thomson, PhD PSM FAcSS FRSA
Professor of *Education*, The University of Nottingham
https://patthomson.net
@ThomsonPat

Books in the Series:

Publishing from your Doctoral Research
Create and Use a Publication Strategy
Janet Salmons and Helen Kara

Making Sense of Academic Conferences

Presenting, Participating and Organising

James Burford and Emily F. Henderson

LONDON AND NEW YORK

Designed cover image: Getty Images

First published 2023
by Routledge
4 Park Square, Milton Park, Abingdon, Oxon OX14 4RN

and by Routledge
605 Third Avenue, New York, NY 10158

Routledge is an imprint of the Taylor & Francis Group, an informa business

© 2023 James Burford and Emily F. Henderson

The right of James Burford and Emily F. Henderson to be identified as authors of this work has been asserted in accordance with sections 77 and 78 of the Copyright, Designs and Patents Act 1988.

All rights reserved. No part of this book may be reprinted or reproduced or utilised in any form or by any electronic, mechanical, or other means, now known or hereafter invented, including photocopying and recording, or in any information storage or retrieval system, without permission in writing from the publishers.

Trademark notice: Product or corporate names may be trademarks or registered trademarks, and are used only for identification and explanation without intent to infringe.

British Library Cataloguing-in-Publication Data
A catalogue record for this book is available from the British Library

ISBN: 978-0-367-69339-8 (hbk)
ISBN: 978-0-367-70169-7 (pbk)
ISBN: 978-1-003-14488-5 (ebk)

DOI: 10.4324/9781003144885

Typeset in Helvetica
by codeMantra

Contents

List of illustrations	viii
List of abbreviations	ix
Acknowledgements	x
About the authors	xi
1 **Introduction: Making sense of academic conferences**	1
2 **Pre-conference: Selecting, preparing, and conference travel**	19
3 **Participating in a conference**	45
4 **Presenting at conferences**	78
5 **Organising conferences**	107
6 **Thinking about conferences**	146
7 **Conclusion**	173
Index	179

Illustrations

1.1	'My first conference' by Rhiannon Nichols	1
2.1	'Conference baggage' by Rhiannon Nichols	19
3.1	'Conferences are (not) holidays' by Rhiannon Nichols	45
4.1	'No input' by Rhiannon Nichols	78
5.1	'Registration desk' by Rhiannon Nichols	107
6.1	'Thinking about conferences' by Rhiannon Nichols	146

Abbreviations

AERA	American Educational Research Association
CFP	Call for papers
CHEER	Centre for Higher Education and Equity Research, University of Sussex
COVID-19	Coronavirus Disease 2019
CV	Curriculum vitae
EDI	Equality, Diversity and Inclusion
FOMO	Fear of missing out
HDMI	High Definition Multimedia Interface
NGO	Non-governmental organisation
NWSA	National Women's Studies Association
Q&A	Question and answer
SARS	Severe Acute Respiratory Syndrome
SIGs	Special Interest Groups
SRHE	Society for Research into Higher Education
UK	United Kingdom
US	United States
VGA	Video Graphics Array

Acknowledgements

The authors would like to thank the series editors of the *Insider Guides to Success in Academia*, Pat Thomson and Helen Kara, for their initial invitation to write this book and for their professionalism and warmth along the way. We would also like to acknowledge the editorial and production teams, including the commissioning editor Sarah Tuckwell, and the anonymous reviewers of the proposal and manuscript. We would like to express our gratitude to Rhiannon Nichols for her wonderful research illustrations.

During the writing process, various readers kindly accepted our invitations to read parts of this manuscript. We want to express our sincere thanks to Jyothsna Belliappa, Mary Eppolite, Marilena Karamatsouki, Georgiana Mihut, Ashley Ng, Chloé Searle, Mareike Smolka, Angelo Tedoldi, Thornchanok Uerpairojkit, Trudie Walters, and Laura Whitburn.

About the authors

James Burford is Assistant Professor of Global Education and International Development at the Department of Education Studies, University of Warwick, UK. He has had academic postings in Thailand, Australia, and the UK in the areas of researcher development and education studies. James is co-editor of the *Conference Inference* blog (https://conferenceinference.wordpress.com/) and has taught about and undertaken research on academic conferences.

Twitter: @jiaburford

Emily F. Henderson is Reader in Gender and International Higher Education in the Department of Education Studies at the University of Warwick, UK. She is co-editor of *Conference Inference* and has been researching conferences since 2011, including the 'In Two Places at Once' project (www.warwick.ac.uk/i2po) and *Gender, Definitional Politics and 'Live' Knowledge Production: Contesting Concepts at Conferences* (Routledge, 2020).

Twitter: @EmilyFrascatore

1 Introduction

Making sense of academic conferences

Figure 1.1 'My first conference' by Rhiannon Nichols

You might overhear people talking about them across the tearoom. An academic in your department might announce that they are searching for student volunteers to help out at one. Your supervisor might suggest that you consider serving on a committee or presenting your own work. But an important question remains: what are academic conferences, and what purpose might they serve? In this book, we have gathered our thoughts on

DOI: 10.4324/9781003144885-1

conferences because we know that these events can be mysterious for newcomers. Across these pages, we hope to assist researchers who are trying to make sense of academic conferences to have some further coordinates to navigate by. In this book, we address what tends to happen at conferences, how new entrants to the world of research might locate and then prepare for an academic conference, and why we believe a thoughtful approach to the roles of delegate, presenter, and organiser of these events is worthwhile.

1.1 What are academic conferences?

If you were to type the word 'conference' into a search engine, you would likely discover a wide array of material, some relevant and some not so much. This is because the word 'conference' is used in so many different contexts and carries many different meanings all at once. For example, there is the *athletic conference*, a grouping of teams who compete against each other in a sports league; the *parent-teacher conference*, where guardians meet their children's teachers and discuss their learning progress; and the *press conference*, which are official events organised to distribute information and to take media questions. These are all quite different events to the *academic conferences* we will be discussing in this book. In a previous encyclopaedia entry, we have described academic conferences as 'planned events for a group of people with a common interest, where participants share and disseminate knowledge' (Henderson & Burford, 2020, p. 289). Critics might accuse us of being a tad vague in offering up such a broad definition! But there's a reason for keeping the category fairly wide: the variance of academic conferences can be massive.

Suppose we were to try to place academic conferences within a broader 'family' of events. In that case, we might imagine them as close cousins to other gatherings that bring people who have a common interest together. Here we might be thinking of industry conferences (which attract industry practitioners) and other related events such as political party conventions, diplomatic gatherings, and activist fora. While it is likely that the primary kind of conference that researchers will attend are academic conferences, some multi-stakeholder events might see researchers rubbing shoulders with activists and advocates, practitioners, politicians, and consumers of services, among others. Academic conferences also share similarities to other research dissemination events that commonly occur within higher education institutions, such as seminars and symposia. However, research seminars and symposia tend to involve fewer speakers and often take place over a shorter duration than conferences do.

The ways in which conference time is organised vary hugely. However, generally speaking, a conference will be split between longer plenary sessions (where all the conference community can gather together), shorter parallel sessions (where people break off into different rooms), and mealtimes (when all delegates often return together). Sometimes, parallel sessions might be organised by special interest groups (SIGs), allowing streams of similar papers to be scheduled together within the larger conference. Plenary sessions are often where keynote speakers will be scheduled. The function of keynote speakers is to address the conference's central theme. They often 'headline' the conference, sometimes acting as a drawcard used on marketing materials for the conference. The term 'keynote' apparently arrives to conferencing from the practice of *a cappella* singing, where a note is played to determine the key in which a song will be sung. Clearly then, it is imagined that keynote speakers will have an important role in shaping the tone and tenor of the conference, and often they are esteemed members of the research community. In practice, keynotes may contribute to this 'tone and tenor' to varying degrees. In addition to either poster presentations or oral presentations, a manner of other kinds of activity might take place at conferences. For example, there might be round table discussion sessions, where presentations may be shorter, and there is greater time for audiences to contribute their opinions. Other events can be scheduled too, ranging from film screenings, book launches and annual general meetings, cultural performances, and workshops, among others. Some conferences schedule poster presentation sessions, where selected researchers bring along a large poster about their research, and conference delegates are given time to peruse the posters and network with the poster presenters. Recent years have also seen the emergence of digital poster sessions, where presenters might be invited to share their posters online, either live or as a pre-recording.

Conferences can also vary hugely in terms of scale. Some events are extremely large. For example, the face-to-face American Educational Research Association (AERA) annual meeting has frequently gathered more than 15,000 attendees each year. In conferences of this scale, attendees will often need to meet across multiple hotels. Other conferences might be medium in size, perhaps able to fit in one hotel or conference centre. And other conferences might be relatively small boutique events, which might attract around 30–100 delegates. Considerations of scale often shape the possible venues in which conferences might occur. While many conferences might occur in hotels, conference or retreat centres, others might take place in universities, turning university teaching rooms into conference rooms and university dormitories into guest accommodation.

1.2 Who organises conferences, and what might their purpose be?

Many groups or individuals may organise conferences, and these groups or individuals organise conferences for different reasons and anticipate various audiences (for more on conference organising, see Chapter 5). Academic associations or learned bodies are key organisations that play a role in organising conferences. These associations seek to steward a particular knowledge discipline at a national or international level. Often these academic associations host regular conferences, which are key gathering points for researchers in the discipline, and where important governance and symbolic matters affecting the research field might be decided upon and conferred (e.g., elections of officeholders, the awarding of scholarships and competitive research funding). And yet not all conferences are organised at this level. Some conferences may also be organised by departments, networks, or research centres within higher education institutions. The organising teams of these conferences are often small collectives of academics who run the conferences on a shoestring budget and donate their time. Often these smaller conferences may have more of a niche focus. An even smaller kind of conference might be organised to facilitate the dissemination of a particular research project or to prepare for or celebrate the publication of an edited book or a journal special issue. Other conferences might be more clearly aligned with researchers' professional development and learning. For example, many higher education institutions create conferences aimed at giving undergraduate or postgraduate researchers a venue to present their emerging research findings. These conferences usually have an explicitly developmental focus, offering students an opportunity to present their findings in a more supported way.

Next is the question of what purpose academic conferences might have. The follow-up question of 'for whom?' might be helpful, as we suspect this answer varies greatly by audience. For researchers themselves, conferences often catalyse the production of papers and presentations, which are then shared with colleagues. Researchers use the opportunity to present to get feedback, which can then help them shape work in progress and to help them prepare for eventual publication. Indeed, some conferences publish a collection of outputs in the form of conference proceedings, which are the written record of presented work. Then again, a conference presentation might be an opportunity to share work that is nearer to completion (particularly in disciplines where researchers may be concerned about protecting intellectual property before publication). Conferences can sometimes result in delegates being invited to publish their work in edited books or special issues of journals, where papers are re-drafted and collated by an editor or group of editors. Research dissemination is not the only reason why researchers attend conferences. Learning is

Introduction: Making sense of academic conferences 7

another. Because conference presentations are often based on work in progress or freshly published work, conference delegates may have the opportunity to learn about ground-breaking work that hasn't yet made it into print.

Across both answers, you can see that attending conferences may be considered a vital part of academic career development. For early career researchers, attending a conference can be understood as a critical professional learning site. Conferences are locations where newcomers are socialised into the field, they enable networks to be developed, and reputations to be built. They also offer opportunities for learning about key players in a field of knowledge and are an important space to learn more about the social practices of 'becoming an academic' in a broader sense. In addition to publishing, conferences are linked with the academic employment market. In some disciplinary and national contexts, they are locations where job interviews are conducted, or equally, connections made at conferences may be important for securing interviews following the conference. Colleagues may let each other know about new or upcoming positions or even headhunt researchers. As you can see with conferences, there is always a lot going on!

1.3 A curiosity with conferences: Our story

Perhaps you are wondering how we ended up writing this book and how we ended up writing it together. It may not surprise you to learn that we first met in the lead up to an academic conference. In 2014, we were both doctoral researchers working in higher education research. Jamie was a distance student studying at Auckland University in New Zealand and living in Thailand, where he had begun his first academic job. Emily was a doctoral researcher based in the UK, examining conferences as a key part of her doctoral study. Emily had been awarded some event funding to convene a symposium and put out a call for papers (CFP), hoping to attract colleagues interested in presenting at the symposium and at the Society for Research into Higher Education (SRHE) Annual Conference in Wales, which would follow shortly thereafter. Jamie and Emily and two of their colleagues, Genine Hook and Vicky Gunn, sent abstracts, which conference reviewers accepted. And so, in December that year, we all went to the SRHE conference to present our work. This was a pivotal meeting for both of us where lots of things seemed to 'click'. Emily describes the event as a moment where she realised the joys of curating academic community at conferences, and Jamie describes a feeling of finally understanding who he might be in conversation with, indeed who the imagined audience he might be writing his doctoral thesis for.

After this session, Jamie returned to Bangkok, and Emily went back to London, but we kept in touch. There was a relevant journal special issue coming out, and we decided to submit a report about the conference and what we had presented there (Burford & Henderson, 2015). Now we had not only met at the conference, but we'd also had a chance to write together, and from there, a friendship blossomed. Over the next couple of years, we cheered from the sidelines as each of us finished PhDs, found new jobs, and moved countries and cities. Fast forward to 2017, and we decided we wanted to

Introduction: Making sense of academic conferences 9

expand our collaboration further by starting an academic blog together. Neither of us can fully remember whose idea it was, but eventually, we landed on conferences as our key topic of interest. In the early months of 2017, the *Conference Inference* blog (https://conferenceinference.wordpress.com/) was born! We hoped *Conference Inference* would be a place for sharing critical and creative thinking around conferences. We came to the blog with the understanding that, despite spending lots of time and money on them, and organising them year after year, many researchers did not plug in their 'researcher brains' when thinking about conferences. We felt that it would be helpful to create a space where scholars could share relevant research on conferences and puzzle through these gatherings from multiple disciplinary perspectives. As editors of the blog, we have now published over 120 posts and hosted over 100 guest writers who have shared their thoughts on conferences. As the blog has continued to grow, we've been astounded by how complex (and sometimes strange) these events can be!

Our interest in academic conferences extends beyond the blog too. We also arrive to write this book as researchers and as teachers of conferences. This book is grounded in research projects that each of us have conducted. Emily undertook her own doctoral study on conferences as sites of international knowledge production in a project called 'Eventful Gender' (Henderson, 2016), and has undertaken follow-up research on care responsibilities and conferences in a study called 'In Two Places at Once' (www.warwick.ac.uk/i2po). Jamie has been part of a cultural history project with colleagues investigating the impact of the International Academic Identities Conference called 'A decade of dialogue' (https://rihe.hiroshima-u.ac.jp/en/research_activities/

10 *Introduction: Making sense of academic conferences*

international-joint/summary/project-2/). You can find links to some of our publications at various points during the book if you are interested in more information. The book also emerges out of a particular pedagogical context, drawing on teaching material that Jamie used in 'How to conference', 'Writing conference abstracts', and 'Being a session chair' workshops that he conducted at La Trobe University (2018–20), and the work Emily undertakes as an academic advisor to her department's Annual Postgraduate Research Conference. Both Jamie and Emily have served on conference committees and have therefore also been involved in the organising of conferences too. We bring all these experiences to the pages of this book.

As individuals who work and study inside universities, there is sometimes a tendency to imagine a certain consistency of experience across disciplines—after all, we often only really see things from our own disciplinary vantage points. However, the ways different disciplines work and the kinds of academic practices that are taken for granted within them can be highly variable. The authors of this book have each taken diverse journeys in and through higher education (between us, we have experience in the disciplines of English literature and modern languages, political science, development studies, gender studies, and education studies); yet as academics, we are primarily social scientists who go to conferences in the field of education. We want readers to be aware of this because some conferences practices (e.g., presenting a poster or reading a pre-written paper out loud) may be extremely common in some disciplines and almost unheard of in others. As with all advice books it is important to filter the material you read here in conversation with experts in your own discipline—these experts will

Introduction: Making sense of academic conferences 11

have a closer understanding of how conferences tend to work in your discipline.

1.4 Why are we writing this book?

Academic conferences can appear to be mysterious events. For emerging researchers, it can seem like those in the know *just know* where to find information about upcoming conferences, what to prepare, and how people tend to behave at them. It can be difficult for those who are not in the know to even figure out where to begin. In writing this book, we hope to offer guidance for folks who are finding their conference feet, to give a better sense of what tends to happen at conferences, and how researchers can make the most of the possibilities they offer for learning and becoming a part of a community of scholars. However, as the title of this book signals, we are not only interested in orienting newcomers to academic conferences. Across this book, we will try and make sense of what conferences might be and the choices we have as to how we act at them.

In order to make sense of conferences, we first need to address some of the various ways that these gatherings tend to arise in academic chatter. Talk about conferences is often split, where on the one hand they are presented as underwhelming, or indeed as leisure trips and holidays. On the other hand, they are presented as 'essential' events for researchers. In this in-between zone, conferences appear as both difficult to recognise as 'real' academic work at the same time as critical spaces where researchers learn, disseminate knowledge, build networks, and form friendships that help sustain an academic life. In writing this book, we hope to step into this confusing space, drawing back the curtain on practices that may be tacit and unexplained and reflecting on the intricacies hidden within these events.

We begin this book with the view that an inquisitive stance towards conferences is valuable. What do online and face-to-face conferences do for scholars and our fields? What role do they play in promoting learning, researcher development, and knowledge production? What are the key differences between online and face-to-face conferences? What are the pleasures and pains of conferences? How can we decode the rituals, mundane and exotic, that go on at them? And at the most basic level, what might we do, and how might we be at them? Our goal is to take a practical tone; after all, we want this book to offer helpful advice for readers. And yet, we also want to couple this with critical provocations. We believe that the norms around conferences ought to be questioned and evaluated rather than simply reproduced. Our overall approach is to discuss conferences from a holistic perspective, thinking through existing issues and debates, but also pushing these further, asking you, the reader, to reflect on the decisions you make—and the decisions that are made for you—in and around conferences.

1.5 The audience for this book and ways to read it

We have written this book for postgraduate researchers and early career academics to help them to make sense of and navigate academic conferences. However, the book may also be of interest to attendees of undergraduate/ Masters conferences, professionals who want to engage

Introduction: Making sense of academic conferences 13

with academic spaces (e.g., hybrid conferences), as well as mentors and supervisors, and researcher developers who are helping students to make sense of these events. Across the book, we use the words 'researchers', 'scholars', 'scientists', and 'academics' interchangeably to recognise some of the different ways people involved in academic conferences might see themselves—but we want to be clear that this book is for anyone who might want to read it! The book is particularly aimed at those going to their first conference. It is essential to clarify that, as authors, we don't position ourselves as 'experts' in how to negotiate conferences or as entirely consistent or flawless subjects who can be looked to as shining beacons of skilful or equitable conferencing. We are ourselves muddling through academic lives, learning, growing, and sometimes messing up.

We have written this book because few books directly address academic conferences from a holistic perspective. Existing books which provide practical information and guidance on conferences tend to focus on one aspect of conferences, such as presenting, posters, networking, or organising conferences. These guides often provide a comprehensive commentary on specific elements of conferencing, and we include many of them in the further reading recommendations at the end of each chapter. Our book differs from these existing works, in that it introduces conferences from a holistic perspective, as can be seen from the chapter summaries below.

Chapter 2, 'Pre-conference: Selecting, preparing, and conference travel', covers questions researchers might contemplate before attending a conference. The chapter outlines steps that researchers can take to determine which conferences are out there, including key sources of advice and support. Next, critical principles for exercising scholarly judgement about the 'right' or 'wrong' conference for an individual researcher are discussed, including concerns about 'predatory conferences'. The chapter then considers securing conference travel funding and introduces common sources to investigate. The next section of the chapter covers pre-conference preparation, including key practices delegates can employ to learn about the conference and polish up their online presence. This section will also cover strategies for managing care work and other responsibilities at home. Finally, the chapter considers key aspects of conference travel, including planning, transportation, safety, and where to stay.

In Chapter 3, 'Participating in a conference', we identify strategies to maximise conference participation. The chapter covers basic preparations such as reading the programme and conference booklet, and more complex questions such as what being a 'good' audience member might mean. The chapter outlines the role of the session chair or discussant, then moves on to a vitally important aspect of conferencing: networking. The chapter outlines suggestions for emerging researchers to network online both before and during the conference—including at online conferences. We don't forget some key topics of enduring interest, such as navigating mealtimes, conference discos and other social events, conference clothing, and ways of reducing our environmental impact at conferences. We also cover key issues that can interrupt conference attendance, including illness, transport issues, and managing care responsibilities. The chapter concludes by considering post-conference activities.

Chapter 4, 'Presenting at conferences', offers an overarching view of the process of presenting at a conference, both from a practical point of view and by raising some

Introduction: Making sense of academic conferences 15

critical questions for presenters to consider. The chapter is divided into sections that focus on different aspects of presenting in chronological order. Conference abstracts are discussed in terms of what they are and which purposes they serve. Various choices about presentations are introduced, including the type of presentation (e.g., oral, poster) and whether/how to include technology in presentations. Techniques for preparing to present are included, in addition to considerations for managing the question and answer (Q&A) session and suggestions for post-presentation follow-up tasks. The chapter gives readers space to question, critique, and even resist, as well as to learn the rules of the game.

In Chapter 5, 'Organising conferences', we turn to practical and critical considerations for organising a conference, referring to this process as 'curating' a conference. Often neglected aspects of conference design are included, such as setting aims and aligning these with the conference pedagogy, leadership style, and ethos. Moving on from the overarching design of the conference, the chapter moves on to choices that need to be made about different formats and elements of the conference and practical considerations for conference organisers. Finally, conference evaluation is addressed. Overall, the chapter argues that conference organising is a complex and multi-faceted process that benefits from an engaged, reflexive approach.

With Chapter 6, 'Thinking about conferences', we hope to tempt those reaching for the book for a specific purpose to devote some additional time to think critically about conferencing practices. The chapter encompasses four sections, each taking a different angle on conferences. First, there is a consideration of conferences in relation to equality, diversity, and inclusion (EDI). Here, conferences are considered as having their own EDI issues, but also as sites whose EDI issues have wider ramifications for the academic profession at large. Second, the chapter moves on to questions of conferences in relation to the democratisation of knowledge production and circulation. Third, the chapter addresses the environmental and sustainability concerns attached to the global conference industry. Finally, the chapter addresses the fragility (and resilience) of conferences.

The book ends with a short conclusion chapter that synthesises the key messages of the book, discusses the contextual specificity of conferences and the lack of universal expectations and experiences. The chapter invites readers to form their own opinion of the suggestions we make and to develop their own conference practices, in community with others.

1.6 Concluding thoughts

In concluding, we want to share our assumptions about what we might be doing together as authors and readers in this book. One of the things you will notice as you continue reading this book is that we hope to both illuminate some of the 'rules of the game', at the same time as we encourage you to question them. Often readers come to books like this one to find answers to a question like 'how to do X'. As authors, we hope there will be practical answers for you within these pages, offering you our take on the multiple ways you could answer the question. However, when we hear the 'how to do X' question in relation to conferences, we often want to respond with a question of our own: what kind of researcher do you want to be? What may seem like 'how to *do*' questions are, in our view, also often 'how to *be*' questions. So, as you read this book, you will also encounter personal and perhaps ethical questions like: who am I? Who do I want to be, for others and myself? Our operating premise in this book is that we not only inhabit the university but that *we are* the university. The university is never just an abstract entity that exists somewhere 'over there'; the university is something we bring into being through our daily decisions and how we choose to show up for each other, including at conferences. This means that we can all play a role in creating the university and indeed the conference we wish to inhabit.

1.7 Further reading: Introducing conferences

- Henderson, E. F. (2020). *Gender, definitional politics and 'Live' knowledge production: Contesting concepts at conferences*. London; New York, NY: Routledge.
- Henderson, E. F., & Burford, J. (2020). 'Conferences'. *Sage Encyclopedia of Higher Education* (290–293)
- Hickson III, M. (2006). Raising the Question #4 why bother attending conferences? *Communication Education, 55*(4), 464–468. doi:10.1080/03634520600917632
- Mair, J. (2014). *Conferences and conventions: A research perspective*. London; New York, NY: Routledge.
- Nicolson, D. J. (2017). *Academic conferences as neoliberal commodities*. Basingstoke: Palgrave Macmillan.
- Rogers, T. (2013). *Conferences and conventions: A global industry* (3rd ed.). Abingdon; New York, NY: Routledge.

References

Burford, J., & Henderson, E. F. (2015). Queer inroads: Two queer higher education symposia reviews written otherwise. *Higher Education Research & Development, 34*(4), 801–807. doi:10.1080/07294360.2015.1058881

Henderson, E. F. (2016). *Eventful gender: An ethnographic exploration of gender knowledge production at international academic conferences.* (PhD). London: UCL Institute of Education.

Henderson, E. F., & Burford, J. (2020). 'Conferences'. In M. E. David & M. J. Amey (Eds.), *Sage Encyclopedia of Higher Education* (pp. 290–293). London: Sage Publications Ltd.

Hickson III, M. (2006). Raising the Question #4 why bother attending conferences? *Communication Education, 55*(4), 464–468. doi:10.1080/03634520600917632

Mair, J. (2014). *Conferences and conventions: A research perspective.* London; New York, NY: Routledge, Taylor & Francis Group.

Rogers, T. (2013). *Conferences and conventions: A global industry* (3rd ed.). Abingdon; New York, NY: Routledge.

2 Pre-conference

Selecting, preparing, and conference travel

Figure 2.1 'Conference baggage' by Rhiannon Nichols

2.1 Introducing pre-conference steps

Attending a conference often looks simple on paper. A researcher needs to get from A to B, hopefully with their luggage and something to present, and then return home (again, hopefully with their luggage!). Or they need to sign in to an online platform, share their screen and—magic—it's all over! But rarely is arriving at a conference

DOI: 10.4324/9781003144885-2

so simple. In the lead up to attending a conference, much information will be collected and sifted through, conversations will occur, and decisions will be taken. This chapter canvasses many key pre-conference considerations that researchers navigate. As such, this chapter may be especially helpful for those who are relatively new to conferencing, or it may also be a valuable resource for mentors who are inducting an emerging scholar into the world of academic gatherings. The chapter covers three critical areas: (i) how to go about selecting a conference, (ii) important pre-conference preparation steps, and (iii) decisions about conference travel for in-person conferences. Across this chapter, we draw on our experiences as conference researchers and advice from other conference veterans to offer a comprehensive orientation to pre-conference planning. And at points, this chapter will extend beyond logistics and to-do lists, opening up conference preparation to critical interrogation. Hopefully, we'll leave the reader some curly questions to consider.

2.2 Learning about conferences in your field

For newcomers, the world of academia can seem anything from alienating to exhilarating, banal to bizarre. There's so much for an emerging researcher to wrap their head around, from new words and theories, new ways of writing, and perhaps new tools and technologies to get the hang of. While some of us may have family members who have been to university or even family members who have been to academic conferences before, for many people, conferences are part of academia's hidden landscape, a

Selecting, preparing, and conference travel 21

terrain full of mysterious people doing mysterious things. For lots of people gearing up to their first conference, it can seem that expert academics glide through seamlessly, while new players struggle to find out where the game is even being played! In this section, we want to help emerging researchers understand how they might figure out about conferences that are out there in their fields.

As we indicated in the introductory section, conferences can vary by size, scope, and organisational structure. As an emerging researcher, it is often valuable to try to map out the different kinds of conferences and symposia opportunities that might be relevant. But how to determine relevance? In thinking about this question, you might begin by considering the contours of your own discipline. Do you study in the discipline of *education*, *geography*, or *physics*? If so, there might be major international and national conferences that bring researchers together from within each one of these disciplines. These conferences are often large and have a wide spread of work represented from across various corners of the discipline. However, not all conferences operate at such a high level. Also, there may be sub-disciplines within each of these fields, where more specific conversations occur. For example, consider *early childhood education*, *human geography*, and *nanotechnology*, or spaces where disciplines converge, for instance, *the geographies of early childhood education.* These conferences are more likely to be smaller and bring together a more narrowly focused group of delegates. However, not all conferences are organised around disciplines or sub-disciplines; some may be organised around themes and topics that are inter- or trans-disciplinary (e.g., COVID-19 or #MeToo) instead. Other conferences may focus on methodologies (e.g., ethnography or arts-based research) or theoretical approaches (e.g., feminist theory). If the first step is getting a clearer idea of the kinds of areas that you are working in as a researcher, the next is to figure out which conferences are out there and what they might offer for your development and the advancement of your research.

Academic supervisors/advisors are often key sources of information about conferences that might be relevant for you. As researchers who have likely been around the academic block a little longer, supervisors may be able to help you think about conferences you might wish to attend. Indeed, this could be a question to raise in a supervision meeting as a part of your wider planning of the various stages of your study. As supervisors, we try to make our conferencing movements visible for students that we work with, so they see the conferences that we attend, present at, or help to organise. But it is also important to remember that the knowledge of supervisors is not limitless! It can be valuable to have conversations with others too in order to map possible conference opportunities that might be relevant for you. In addition to supervisors, you might pay attention to the conferences that other senior colleagues in your area go to or ask your peers about what conferences they recommend. The key message here is: as an emerging researcher, you aren't expected to know everything already! It's perfectly acceptable to ask other researchers for guidance and to bring these deliberations out into the open about where you will invest your time, resources, and networking energies.

One of the challenges with learning about the conferences in your field is that new conferences are constantly popping up. This happens because fields are ever-changing as new areas emerge and new questions become urgent. This is part of what makes research so exciting! But it is also a conundrum. How can researchers keep on top of a rapidly expanding list of conference opportunities? One valuable source of information for emerging researchers exists online. Some researchers might begin by looking at conference alert websites that separate conferences by discipline and geographical area. However, be careful with these resources as searching in these ways might offer too many results to be of use. Perhaps the best way to use these websites is to develop a shortlist that you can then use to undertake further online investigations, and to do this in discussion with more experienced researchers. Another valuable way of learning about conference opportunities is by ongoing participation in digital academic spaces that proliferate on Facebook, Twitter, LinkedIn, or academic blogs. Suppose you join academic groups on Facebook, follow other academics on Twitter or LinkedIn, search through hashtags relevant to your area of research (e.g., #CritEvents, #AcWri), or regularly engage with academic blogs. In so doing, you are likely to bump into different calls for conference papers (CFP), or other researchers talking about conferences that you might be interested in. Another fundamental way to identify possible conferences is to join disciplinary electronic mailing lists, sometimes known as listservs. Often researchers will post conference opportunities to these mailing lists, so this can be a good way of keeping on top of conference opportunities that are coming up.

2.3 Selecting a conference to attend

Once you have found a conference, or several conferences, that you might be interested in attending, it is time to exercise careful judgement about the best conference for you. These are difficult decisions for any researcher to make, and sometimes the value of a given conference can only really be known through trial and error. However, at the outset of this section, it is important to note that no 'selection' of a conference to attend is entirely free; it is inevitably shaped by a variety of opportunities and constraints that each of us has as a conference delegate.

The first thing to note about selecting a conference to attend is that this judgement is often nestled inside a wider process of strategic decision-making that you might make about your development as a researcher and your desires for communicating the results of your project. For readers who are graduate researchers or post-doctoral fellows, you will likely have a more or less clear timeline ahead of you in terms of your project and its key milestones. This offers you opportunities to plan when you might want to attend conferences and what material you might have to share at them. For advisors and supervisors reading this book, it can be helpful to sit down with researchers you are working with to plan out the budget and timelines of a project and to help researchers to determine how many conferences they might budget for and when it might be best in the project cycle to attend them. While it is helpful to have a rough sense of what might be possible and to draft in possible conferences to attend, it may equally be unwise to lock things down too early. Conferences are unpredictable beasts, and while we can generally assume that an annual conference might happen once a year, many other factors are challenging to plan for, such as the location of the conference or its cost in several years' time. The COVID-19 pandemic has also demonstrated that even annual conferences which tend to operate like clockwork are vulnerable to disruption. Despite the uncertainties, once you have done some

Selecting, preparing, and conference travel 25

'bigger picture' planning around conferences, you will be better positioned to evaluate when conference opportunities pop up.

Some of the decisions you may wish to make concern strategies around 'tapping in' to particular kinds of research conversations. Remember that different kinds of researchers will gather at different types of conferences, and the conversations you have access to at a conference will be particular to those delegates. So, it's worth thinking about what conversations you might need *now* at this point in your research process. Think about how what you have to say and what others have to share might be shaped by going to a particular conference. For example, when Jamie was making decisions about what conferences he wanted to attend as a doctoral student, he tried to pursue a mix of interests, including wider discipline conferences (e.g., Education, Higher Education, Sociology), sub-field conferences (e.g., Doctoral Education, Supervision, Gender and Education), as well as more narrow conversations (e.g., Academic Identity), and on methodologies (e.g., Ethnography) and theory (e.g., Queer Theory). If you are also undertaking a more extended programme of research work (like a PhD), you might consider whether some mix of higher level and more focused conversations would be the best combination for you, or whether your goal is to 'commit' to a regular conference and establish relationships with attendees over several years.

It's not only *what* you might want to talk about and listen to, but also the size and organisation of the conference shapes *how* those conversations might ultimately play out. Perhaps an early decision you might make is deciding between modes: are you keen to go to online, in-person or hybrid events? There are many factors to weigh up here. Perhaps you have caring responsibilities that you cannot or do not wish to separate yourself from, and an online conference might be the best choice for you. Another key consideration for selecting a conference is the financial horizon that you may be working with. Academic conferences, and associated travel and accommodation costs, can be expensive, so the price may be a critical deciding factor in making your judgement (there is more on conference funding in the section that follows). Perhaps you decide that you would prefer to meet face-to-face. In this case, consideration of scale may be a deciding factor for you. Maybe you are keen to experience a 'mega-conference' associated with your field, where 10,000 delegates might converge across several different hotels in one city. Or perhaps you want to attend a 'boutique' conference which may have fewer than 100 delegates. Another thing to remember in making your decision is that conferences also have their own vibes. Some conferences are stuffier and more conservative; others are more edgy or informal. Sometimes we can pick up this vibe from the promotional material on the conference website, the conference theme that is set (i.e., a particular topic or idea that has a spotlight shone on it across the conference). Other times we might notice things about the conference chair and committee (i.e., those leading the conference) or the keynotes selected to speak. However, sussing out what kind of conference it will be is often difficult. This difficulty can arise because you might be new to the community, but it is also difficult because the 'vibe' of the conference is also produced by the people who show up at it, something which cannot be entirely predicted until the conference itself plays out! This is something that those familiar with conferences may recognise. Because conferences involve repetitions

Selecting, preparing, and conference travel 27

and reiterations, some ways of being together will begin to endure. Yet, in each instance of a conference, a particular community gathers, and because of this each conference is unique—and unpredictable.

A further thing that emerging researchers ought to be aware of is 'predatory conferences'—that is, conferences that may not be conferences at all or for-profit conferences whose primary aim is to make researchers part with large sums of cash without offering much academic substance in return. Conferences that may be classed as 'predatory' are those which may misrepresent the editorial oversight the conference has (i.e., claims of peer review, but all papers are simply accepted to collect fees), or those which advertise things (e.g., locations where the conference will take place, presenter identities) which are not true. Predatory conferences can sometimes be easy to spot. Perhaps you, a researcher in the field of ethnomusicology, receive an email inviting you to present your work at a conference on medical technology. Seems a bit suspect, doesn't it? In fact, for many of us, our spam folders already groan under the weight of the more dubious of these invitations. Other predatory conferences can be quite savvy. Sometimes they might invite an academic to give a keynote, only to ask that person to pay a fee for the honour. Some predatory operators even create websites that almost completely mirror another conference's name, location, and dates, hoping to trick folks who have accidentally stumbled across a link to the wrong website. In other cases, predatory conferences may occur, and established scholars may find themselves present at or even help organise them without knowing that they are helping a suspicious operator. If you have doubts, discuss the conference with your supervisors or other colleagues. If you have serious doubts about the conference, you might check with the venue where the conference is being held (if the hotel has no record of the conference, this might sound alarm bells). Also, you might want to write directly to the organiser of a legitimate conference to let them know that another conference is trying to prey on their pool of would-be delegates. If you have concerns that a conference you are interested in may be a predatory conference, it may be helpful to check it against these criteria developed by James McCrostie (https://scholarlyoa.files.wordpress.com/2016/06/proposed-criteria-for-identifying-predatory-conferences.pdf). It is worth noting, however, that sometimes these conferences can be really hard to spot even for experienced researchers—so there is no need to feel ashamed if you have become inadvertently caught up in one.

Other factors might not seem as academic as those listed above, but they are often important in shaping decision-making about conference attendance. For example, sometimes the geographical location of the conference really matters. Maybe you will jump at the chance to go to a conference in New Zealand because that's where your family live, or perhaps you have always wanted to go rock climbing in Thailand and will take the opportunity after the conference. It might be the case that you are travelling with an accompanying spouse and your partner's dream is to ride on the Shinkansen fast trains in Japan. Whatever the case may be, these personal motivations are often factored into conference decision-making for researchers, who are human beings after all.

On the flip side, geographical places may be less desirable for you, perhaps for their extreme climate, the safety of the location, or difficulties associated with travel there. Equally, we need to be careful about using language like 'choice' and 'judgement' as though these are neutral and similarly available for all. For some delegates, border restrictions or significant impediments need to be accounted for when 'choosing' a conference. These border restrictions disproportionately impact scholars from the Global South seeking to attend conferences in the Global North, who may face steep visa costs, long distances to travel to seek a visa or be denied the possibility due to an inability to secure a visa. These impediments are not just unfortunate for the individual academics involved; they also impoverish knowledge production for all. The fact is, for a healthy and thriving global research culture, we need contributions from colleagues from all around the world. Other colleagues may not be able to 'choose' a given conference because it is inaccessible. Researchers with a disability have long called out for the need to ensure that conference organisers account for accessibility when designing conference events and booking conference venues (see Chapter 6).

There will be ethical decisions involved for some researchers regarding which conferences they might attend. These ethical decisions could be related to, for example, concerns about climate change and the desire to participate in online conferences or those which are accessible via train as opposed to long-haul flights. Other researchers make ethical decisions about the composition of the keynotes—perhaps choosing to avoid conferences that perpetuate 'manels' (all man panels) or 'whanels' (all white panels) as invited speakers. Some researchers decide to boycott particular conferences that invite controversial speakers who might use their platform to share polemic messages about others. Other people choose to avoid conferences with a bad record of handling complaints such as racial discrimination or sexual harassment. Other researchers decide to avoid conferences in particular countries where there are academic boycotts in response to particular government policies or in solidarity with oppressed minorities. As you can see, there are often many decisions that go into deciding on whether or not to attend a particular conference.

2.4 Conference funding

Once you have made some judgements about what kind of conferences you might wish to attend, it is important to think through how to fund your conference participation. Some of us work or study in institutions where conference funding is readily available, others already know that there is limited (if any) funding support. In this section, we will consider options for folks in all of these situations.

If there is conference support available, to secure such funding researchers often need to prepare proposals well in advance of the conference date. This means that careful planning across the research project is vital. In searching for conference funding, it can be helpful to learn to 'read' your higher education institution. For example, your institution might be divided up between central units and other administrative units (e.g., a faculty that contains many different schools, which, in turn, have separate departments/research centres). The language that is used at your institution might differ. In broad terms, it might be helpful to look for institution-wide sources of conference funding (i.e., those held at the central level of an institution), and funding schemes held at the more 'local' level, closer to the researcher. Sometimes conference support might be clearly marked as such; other times, you could look for sources of funding that refer to 'travel', such as travel bursaries for those with caring responsibilities. It is also important to note that the approval for conference funding at many institutions may depend upon your acceptance of an oral presentation or a poster at a conference. While delegates can attend a conference without presenting themselves, this is less commonly funded by institutions.

In addition to these sources of support that your institution might manage, you may be able to access project funding (i.e., funding secured as part of a funded research project). If you are a graduate researcher working on a funded project, your supervisors will likely be the best people to talk to in order to think through your options. Scholarly associations and learned societies themselves sometimes offer other funding opportunities. However, such scholarships may only be provided to association members, leading to unexpected joining costs. Some of these associations offer grants to disadvantaged or early career scholars or provide discounted rates. Indeed, it may be worth investigating the price of joining the association if this leads to a discount on conference attendance fees. If you are in the position of wanting to attend a conference but are lacking funds to do so, it is worth reaching out to the organisers of the conference to see if you can come to some arrangement. In the past, Jamie worked as a volunteer at a conference, helping to upload slides and ferry trays of muffins around the venue, and was in return able to attend the conference for free. Emily has served as a lead assessor of submissions for a stream at an association conference and received reimbursement for part of the registration fee. Another source of funding that researchers might look out for is external travel grants. These funding sources exist in various places, including those managed by government departments, professional networks, or associations you might be part of, or local service and philanthropic organisations.

A final source to consider is self-funding. When self-funding, researchers need to make careful judgements about their budgets and assess the possible value of the conference opportunity. Remember that the cost of in-person conferences stretches out beyond the registration fee, and may include travel costs, visa costs, accommodation and meals, and local transit costs. To help judge whether self-funding is 'worth it', it can be helpful to reflect on your own goals: are there people going to the conference you definitely want to meet? What stage are you at in your project? Is now the right time? Will you have opportunities to attend a similar conference later paid for by funders? How exciting is the travel opportunity itself? In general terms, the 'return on investment' for conferences is unpredictable. Sometimes we can have career-changing or even life-changing experiences; other times, watching paint dry might offer more excitement. Given this unpredictability, it may be unwise to take on large debts to self-fund a conference. However, in addition to self-funding, there are other options that might help to partly cover travel costs. For example, one might combine conference travel with other activities such as visiting a local department, giving a guest lecture, running a workshop, or undertaking research with a local colleague. In some cases, part of the conference costs (e.g., travel costs) may be defrayed by these other activities. If you are looking for such a connection, your supervisors may help facilitate this.

A final point to note on funding is that, no matter what your funding arrangements, attending in-person conferences is seldom 'free'. There are often hidden costs which may include buying new clothes or luggage, paying for meals out that may be more expensive than the meals at home, or unclaimable expenses such as local transfers or additional care support. It can be valuable to try to factor in some of these costs when making conference decisions, so that they don't come as a surprise later on.

2.5 Preparing for a conference

Having selected a conference and organised funding to support attendance, there remain some further pre-conference preparations to consider. Before a conference, the first thing you might do is some reflection and goal setting. What is it that you want to get out of this particular conference? Is this a chance to showcase some cutting-edge work that you have undertaken? Do you want to attend important sessions that might help shape your thinking on a piece of work or your field at large? Are you gathering information that you will then share with your supervision team or lab group? Do you want to prioritise the networking opportunities that the conference may facilitate (which may even mean skipping the odd session in order to have longer conversations)? Some of the goals you set might be more personal goals. For the shy delegates amongst us, perhaps a goal is to try and talk to one new person each day. For the go-getters, perhaps a goal is to slow down and listen carefully. Others might have goals around well-being and self-care, which might mean wanting to take breaks during the day, drink lots of water, and skip the conference disco to get an early night. There is no perfect way to 'be' at conferences, but noticing the desires you have at the outset can help to shape some of the personal decisions you take as conference participants (see Chapter 3).

One of the things that you can do as delegates before the conference is to look closely at the list of participants and the book of conference abstracts/papers that may be sent to delegates before the conference itself. Doing this reading from the comfort of home (or perhaps the plane or train ride) can be helpful, allowing you to develop a draft conference itinerary in advance, so you aren't wading through screeds of information in the prime networking spots of the conference itself. Once you have an idea of the kinds of talks and sessions you might want to attend, you also have the opportunity to research the presenters in those sessions. Perhaps you might look over their bio on their institutional website, check them out on Twitter or pick out a key article or two to read to get a feeling for the kind of work they do. Such preparations are helpful, not only because they help you make some quick judgements about who you might be interested in networking with, but also because they give you something to talk about when it comes to the networking sessions of the conference (see Chapter 3). Some other helpful steps to undertake prior to setting off for the conference may be checking out the conference hashtag on Twitter and letting others who are following the hashtag know that you are intending to come along to the conference, making sure to tag the conference hashtag and any official conference account when you tweet. Another tip for pre-conference preparation is ensuring that your online digital academic identity is up to date. You might want to (a) create or (b) revise your online profiles (e.g., institutional website, ResearchGate, Academia, LinkedIn, Twitter account) to ensure your affiliations are current, in case people go looking for you.

Managing care responsibilities is another area of much activity prior to attending a conference (see Henderson, 2019a). Some of us may need to make arrangements to ensure care for our friends, partners, family members, or pets. By their very nature, conferences often cause profound disruptions to our lives and the lives of those who depend upon us for their care, and research has demonstrated that those who have care responsibilities are much less likely to access conference opportunities. The absence of carers from conferences has profound equity implications, particularly for academic women who continue to shoulder disproportionate care loads compared to academic men. In recognition of these disruptions, universities and conference organisers have increasingly put in place initiatives to increase the accessibility of conferences for carers, such as care bursaries. Each care bursary scheme will facilitate different things, with some helping to partly cover the cost of enabling the person or people you care for to accompany you to the conference, and others helping to meet the cost of care at home. This judgement about being accompanied versus staying behind is often one of the first decisions that delegates need to make. While some conferences offer a creche and/or designated breastfeeding space, it is important to note that most childcare is provided for non-disabled and young children with much less 'at conference' care offered for other dependents. If you have decided that your dependents will not accompany you to the conference, it may be helpful to explain to loved ones what conferences are all about. For many family members, attending conferences might seem to be a holiday rather than essential work travel. It may be helpful to explain to family members the intensity of conferences and their significance, in order for them to understand why they may be worth all the disruption that they cause. Another key thing that many who manage care responsibilities while at conferences note is the importance of not only Plan Bs but also Plan Cs. What happens if the babysitter falls through, or the person who promised to feed the cat or deliver groceries to an elderly relative can't make it? Lining up these multiple sources of support before attending the conference can make the conference experience itself less stressful—the plan is there, no stressful improvisation is required. A final thing to note on care is that it may not be worth attending the conference if care arrangements are not in place. Perhaps the least desirable option is to make it all the way to the conference only to spend most of your time checking in and managing complex care scenarios from a distance. Such a situation means we are not only far away from those who we love and care about, but we also may not be able to fully participate in the conference we have made so much effort to travel to.

2.6 Getting ready to go: Considerations for conference travel

In the final section of this chapter, we zoom in to consider key aspects of travel to in-person conferences. Preparing for conference travel involves making the same kinds of decisions as preparing for other types of travel, such as holidays. Moreover, conference travel requires the traveller to work, and this is a type of work that many of us find challenging and stressful. This means that we might want to give some careful attention to our travel itinerary, budgeting in time for recovery from flights and any associated jetlag where possible. Both of us have made the mistake of travelling a long way to a conference and have arrived so exhausted that we could not fully participate in all its offerings. We gently suggest that it may be unwise to travel halfway around the world only to spend most of your time in a hotel bed! Many of the other key things that surround all types of travel also apply to conference travel. Some of us will need to secure visas for travel, which may involve asking for invitation letters from conference organisers and approval letters from the institutions where you work and study. It is well worth embarking on visa arrangements as early as possible to avoid disappointment if there are delays. Your institution may have a preferred travel supplier, paperwork to fill in, and requirements surrounding travel insurance, so it is worth asking your supervisors for the institutional particulars.

Conference travellers are often presented with a number of choices about where to stay. When conferences are held at a hotel, it is usually possible to stay at the conference venue, and often this accommodation is offered at special rates for conference delegates (although it may still be expensive). The conference organisers also tend to signal other hotels nearby that they recommend. These judgements about where to stay are up to the individual conference-goer. But some considerations you might want to think about include the value of staying nearby to the venue and the possibilities it opens up for socialising following on from the conference. It can be quite enjoyable to drift from the formal conference sessions to a local cafe, bar, or restaurant with a mob of your conference colleagues. Others might decide that that kind of socialising is precisely what they do not want and may choose to stay a bit further out to afford some privacy to recover from the exertions of a long day of conferencing. Other key questions here are cost, and sometimes staying further away from the venue can be more affordable than in the centre of things. Some key things to consider are whether the accommodation has the facilities you need to minimise discomfort and for you to arrive ready for 'work'. Is there an iron if you need to iron a shirt, or a hairdryer if that is an integral part of putting your look together? These may seem like minor details from afar. But in the moment, a crumpled shirt and wet hair can feel rather stressful when one is trying to impress an intellectual crush or potential future employer. Sometimes, you might need to decide whether to stay with other colleagues who are also attending the conference. For example, many institutions have policies that do not allow supervisors and students to stay in the same room. Jamie has had wonderful experiences travelling and staying with other academics at conferences, sometimes in large apartments with others and other times sharing a single hotel room to cover costs. Travelling as a group can be a lovely way to navigate a new space and can offer opportunities to debrief and make sense of conference sessions. However, these decisions are again made within a constellation of factors, including your budget, your desires for privacy or intimacy, and the nature of your relationship with the travellers in question.

Safety is another key consideration to be factored into travel plans. Often, conference-goers might research an area where they are hoping to stay to get a sense of how safe it may be or any particular precautions to take. But often, this local knowledge is tacit and may not be easily found via a quick internet search. Some things that delegates can do to enhance their safety regarding conference

Selecting, preparing, and conference travel 39

travel include making a 'travel buddy', someone else who is going to the conference who can help you navigate new surroundings, particularly if you are jetlagged. Letting others at home know where you are going can be helpful if you are travelling alone, particularly if you are planning to go sightseeing or stray from the conference programme. Some conference travellers download helpful apps (e.g., translation apps, currency conversion apps) or pre-programme key contacts into their phones in case difficulties arise. Other key steps may include going to a travel doctor to ensure you have all the medications you may need and make sure you have had any recommended vaccines. Some practical steps include checking that your phone data will be accessible to you once you arrive or planning to get an international sim card, and checking with your bank to ensure that your bank card won't be blocked if you use it abroad. It might also be worth travelling with some local currency. Once, while overseas attending a conference, Jamie was mugged, and his credit card was stolen. Thankfully, he was travelling with friends and had carried enough cash to get him through until the end of the trip. While most of the time travel to conferences may not be so dramatic, it is important to note that unexpected things do happen. Your journey may be disrupted by a global pandemic or a volcano spewing ash and lava. There may be adverse weather events, a strike, lost, or stolen luggage. While it is impossible to prepare for all possible threats, some forethought about what you might do in an emergency can be worthwhile to give you peace of mind.

Deciding what clothing you will wear is another key part of conferencing, whether travelling to a conference or attending online. Generally speaking, conferences are described as events where delegates wear 'business casual' attire. However, there might be parts of the conference where formal clothing is called for (e.g., a conference dinner or awards ceremony), or informal clothing is expected (e.g., a walking trip). The conference organisers often specify this in the information they send to delegates. Plenty of websites and blog posts boldly claim to tell newcomers to conferences 'what to wear'. However, we find such advice often tends to reproduce the problematic idea that there is a normative standard that all delegates should aim to follow. While it might be helpful in broad terms to understand what the norms of conference attire are, this does not mean that all delegates can or will wish to live up to this norm, and we don't think it is helpful to reproduce an idea that it is appropriate to police the clothing choices of others. Some delegates might be prioritising comfort; others may be prioritising modesty, whether for cultural or religious reasons. There are many other possibilities, too; for example, delegates might be dressing in congruence with their gender identities, making a political statement, desperate to try out that new pair of shoes or pink pantsuit, and so on. An area where it does seem sensible to listen to the advice of others, is around considerations of cultural appropriateness and climate. For example, Jamie went to a conference in Thailand where delegates were asked to dress in black as part of the nationwide mourning period for the late king Bhumibol Adulyadej which all universities were expected to participate in. To demonstrate respect for your hosts, you might also seek to learn whether some kinds of clothing or the exposure of certain parts of the body are likely to be regarded as inappropriate and make decisions about what you pack in accordance with your own stance in relation to these ideas. Another key consideration is climate—take a look at the range of

Selecting, preparing, and conference travel 41

temperatures and weather conditions likely for the time of year you are visiting and pack accordingly!

Finally, we want to comment on some of the choices that researchers might make about how to be a 'good guest', especially when travelling abroad or participating in a conference at home that is situated in a cultural context unfamiliar to you. In preparing for conference travel, you have the opportunity to do some pre-reading about the context you are travelling to and any of the customs that might be commonly practised in that place. Some of these differences might be customs surrounding greeting and welcome. For example, in conferences in Aotearoa New Zealand, honoured guests may be greeted with a *pōwhiri* or welcome ceremony by the people of the land. This ceremony has its own protocols around appropriate attire and may call upon guests to sing or speak to support the process. Or, in Australia, an Indigenous elder may pay guests the honour of welcoming them to country at the beginning of the conference. Equally, when presenters begin their talks in Australia, they often begin with an acknowledgement of country, which pays respect to the Traditional Owners of that land and acknowledges them as ongoing custodians of the land. Other differences revolve around customs about food or alcohol; for example, in Thailand, it is uncommon for alcohol to be served at academic events, and there may be laws or institutional regulations which prohibit this. Hopefully, coming prepared will help stop you rushing to judgement if something is different to how you would be used to it. We suggest that all of this is a part of the learning of the conference, how to 'be' with colleagues in other parts of the world. This doesn't mean that it is never acceptable for a guest to complain. But it is wise to think carefully about whether the complaint is coming from a place of privilege, how much scope your hosts have to accommodate the request, and how local people might receive it. Learning more about the place you will be travelling to can put you in a better position to navigate these different customs more sensitively.

Being a 'good guest' can also extend to a desire to create as little waste as possible at an in-person conference. While the organisers themselves take many sustainability decisions that impact on the waste produced at conferences, individual delegates have a role to play here too. For example, you might decide to pack a refillable water bottle and a keep cup for hot drinks to save on any disposable cups that might otherwise be wasted. You could also pack a portable plate, cutlery, and coffee stirrer for the same purpose. Although it can be tempting to overindulge at buffets, only serving yourself what you need at each snack break can make an impact on ensuring there is not a lot of wasted food that then needs to be discarded. You might decline the offer of complimentary venue-provided stationery or notebook and bring your own name tag or lanyard. Other sustainability choices include reusing shower towels rather than using a fresh one each day, and selecting to walk or use public transport where possible. You might also ask at the venue where leftover catering ends up, and whether there are options to donate leftover food to those who might need it. It's also important to not make hasty judgements of others, who may be weighing up environmental choices against other kinds of sustainability (e.g., financial or time). It's important to remember that not all participants have the same privileges and may enjoy or need some of the conference luxury that is provided.

***

Selecting, preparing, and conference travel 43

The aim of this chapter has been to open up the process of figuring out the conference landscape, including the steps researchers might take to evaluate a wide selection of possible conference opportunities. We have also sought to survey some of the key considerations that surround preparing for conferences, including conference travel, as well as interrogating some of the political baggage that conference-goers bring with them as they travel. We hope that our discussion of concerns such as passport privilege, gendered care responsibilities, and accessibility, among others, has helped to crack open conference preparation as an interesting area to spend more time thinking about. As we have shown across this chapter, there are many things we can do to prepare ourselves for conferences, and many of us develop our own conference routines or rhythms, with particular bags and objects on standby, or where certain months are pencilled into a calendar each year because they are associated with annual events. Yet, because travelling to conferences involves so many moving parts, there is always the possibility of turbulence and unpredictability. Even experienced conference-goers can be thrown off course or rattled by the rigours of travel. This chapter reminds readers that conferences involve embodied knowledge production, fleshy researcher bodies who ache and tire, feel fear and anxiety, bodies that are vulnerable to the threats many travellers face. And yet, conference bodies are also open to excitement, desire, surprise, and delight.

2.7 Further reading: Pre-conference

- Edelheim, J. R., Thomas, K., Åberg, K. G., & Phi, G. (2018). What do conferences do? What is academics'

intangible return on investment (ROI) from attending an academic tourism conference? *Journal of Teaching in Travel & Tourism, 18*(1), 94–107. doi:10.1080/15313220.2017.1407517
- McCrostie, J. (2018). Predatory conferences: A case of academic cannibalism. *International Higher Education, 2*(93), 6–8. doi:10.6017/ihe.0.93.10425
- McCulloch, A. (2018). Dress codes and the academic conference: McCulloch's iron laws of conferences. *Australian Universities' Review, 60*(1), 50–53.
- Tribe, R. & Marshall, C. (2020). Preparing a conference, doctoral or professional presentation. *Counselling Psychology Review, 35*(2), 30–39.
- Uysal, H. (2021). Getting from point A to point B: Practical tips for seeking conference travel grants. *SSTESOL Journal, 14*(1), 68–70.

References

Henderson, E. F. (2019a). Academics in two places at once: (Not) managing caring responsibilities at conferences. In R. Finkel, B. Sharp, & M. Sweeney (Eds.), *Accessibility, Inclusion, and Diversity in Critical Event Studies* (pp. 218–229). London; New York, NY: Routledge.

McCrostie, J. (2018). Predatory conferences: A case of academic cannibalism. *International Higher Education, 2*(93), 6–8. doi:10.6017/ihe.0.93.10425

McCulloch, A. (2018). Dress codes and the academic conference: McCulloch's iron laws of conferences. *Australian Universities' Review, 60*(1), 50–53.

Uysal, H. (2021). Getting from point A to point B: Practical tips for seeking conference travel grants. *SSTESOL Journal, 14*(1), 68–70.

3 Participating in a conference

Figure 3.1 'Conferences are (not) holidays' by Rhiannon Nichols

3.1 Being there at the conference

As discussed in the previous chapter, it can take a whole lot of effort to get to a conference. All the selecting and exploring of opportunities, all the booking, and packing, and re-packing; all the juggling of other life

DOI: 10.4324/9781003144885-3

commitments. Given that so much effort goes into getting to conferences, it seems worthwhile to spend some time considering how to make the most out of being there. This chapter focuses on strategies that delegates can play with in order to maximise conference participation and suck the most juice possible out of the entire conference experience. Notice the word 'play' here, as this is the spirit with which this chapter proceeds. Rather than offering would-be conference-goers a list of to-dos which might aim to turn you into some kind of 'super-delegate', the goal of this chapter is instead to bring you into contact with different ways you might think of yourself 'being there', perhaps even different ways you might show up *as* yourself *for* yourself. As authors, we wish to make it clear: perfection isn't possible, or even desirable! We want to help you to think about who and how *you* might be, with your personality, identity, ethical commitments, and orientation to academia. We say this because academia needs all kinds of people, not only uber-confident super-networkers.

3.2 Reading the conference booklet, website and programme, and planning your time

Ask anyone who has organised a conference and they'll probably tell you that much careful (often frustrating, painstaking, and unglamorous) work has gone into seemingly mundane things, such as developing a conference website, producing a conference booklet and plotting out the full conference programme (for more on this, see Chapter 5 on Organising conferences). These texts have been workshopped by committees of academics and graduate students, drafted and re-drafted to check the tone is right and the information is solid. The reason that so much careful work goes into these texts is because they are meaningful sources of information for conference delegates. The conference website often goes up long before the conference itself, sometimes functioning to market the conference. The website contains key information about the dates and location of the conference, the organisers' names and affiliations, confirmed keynote speakers, and perhaps recommendations for where to stay, what to do, and where to eat nearby. Usually, after a delegate registers for a conference, there are regular email updates. It might be wise to make sure these messages aren't being filtered into your spam folder. Before contacting the conference organising team directly, it is wise to check the website to see if the answer to your question has already been anticipated. If the organisers haven't anticipated your question, it is a good idea to ask, as many other delegates might have similar queries!

In addition to the conference website, another key resource for planning out how to participate in a conference is the conference booklet. These come in many forms. While historically these booklets were often printed for delegates to collect upon registration at the venue, in many cases now booklets are emailed in advance, downloadable from a conference website, or are available via an app, a link to which is commonly sent to delegates prior to the beginning of the conference. Like the website, the conference booklet is a good source of information for conference delegates. The conference booklet tends to include a statement about the key themes of the conference, details about the keynote speakers, and an overall timetable for the conference. Sometimes there will be reminders about key information such as speaking times, Wi-Fi passwords, or how to upload any presentations prior to a session. The booklet also covers information about the organising team and any sponsors that have supported the event. Just like academics who express exasperation when their carefully prepared syllabus is ignored by students, a similar feeling might arise for conference organisers when delegates neglect to read the conference booklet! It is often well worth the reading time in order to understand the vision of the conference and to soak up other key information. Jamie and Emily take different approaches to reading the conference booklet. Jamie likes to try to read the booklet before he arrives, or at least on the way to the venue so he feels well prepared. Emily, on the other hand, often cannot read while travelling because she gets motion sickness! She likes to arrive at the venue, have a coffee, and read the booklet. She sees it as a way of arriving and settling into the conference space.

With the conference website or conference booklet as key tools, delegates are able to plot out unique conference itineraries, especially for conferences where there are sessions running in parallel. This is one of the joys of conferences, they are a 'pick your own adventure' kind of activity! It is also one of the challenges, rife with micro-decisions and a fair share of FOMO (fear of missing out). When thinking of which sessions to attend, it can be helpful to return to the intention for attending the conference in the first place. Are you going to the conference on a mission to build up knowledge that may be valuable for your research project? If so, it can be valuable to think about the multiple dimensions of the project, including the subject matter, theoretical influences shaping, and your methodological approach. Maybe you can develop a conference itinerary that touches on aspects of each of these areas. However, you might have a different intention for attending the conference. Perhaps you are a practitioner, and you are hoping to encounter real-world applications that are being shared, or maybe you are simply seeking to build up a broad base of knowledge within your wider field. Perhaps you are attending the conference with the goal of finding a new job or meeting a potential doctoral supervisor, in which case you might want to think carefully about which sessions you don't want to miss and ensure you are making the most of the networking sessions. Your own interest in the session (e.g., its speaker list, focus area, and type of session) is usually a good guide, and it might help you to be a more active audience member too. Other considerations for picking your conference itinerary may include the arrangement and location of the sessions. In many smaller conferences, there may not be a significant distance from one session to another, however, in larger venues this can make session-hopping (i.e., moving between streamed rooms) stressful, if not impossible.

There may be a temptation to be extremely virtuous when deciding what sessions to attend, and for delegates to plan to only attend sessions that appear to have a clear correlation with their own objectives. While a laudable intention, this can also lead to a dull conference! Sometimes what we seek from our conference experience is to be surprised, entertained, or taken beyond our niche; sometimes we meet a fascinating person and want to drift into their session to hear more, or the opposite may occur where the 'super star' speaker turns out to be rude during morning tea and we want to give them a wide berth. Events sometimes happen at a conference (e.g., a ferocious incident in the Q&A) where we feel we need to change our plans and 'show up' with our bodies to show support for a new friend, or bear witness, or intervene with questions for a person or a political or intellectual cause we believe in. Maybe you are nosy about how a particular celebrity speaker in your field presents and you want to sit in and find out. In short, it is wise to have a good sense of what is on offer and to use some discernment about which sessions to attend—a solid conference itinerary is seldom developed by wafting hither and thither. But perhaps it is also important to not nail everything down too early—this might prevent the wonders that whims can bring.

Another reason that it's advisable to read through the conference programme in advance is so that you have a sense of the key sessions you are interested in attending, as well as any lulls of activity where you might rest and recover, contact loved ones, check on care arrangements or schedule meetings with colleagues. Conferences can be exhausting events, so often conference organisers programme in these lulls, with morning and afternoon breaks and long mealtimes. Where possible, one might plan in meetings with colleagues during these times, or after the conference activities have concluded. While it might seem like the 'correct' thing to do to fill up all the conference time with sessions in the formal programme, it is also helpful to appreciate that some of the most important conference work may happen when delegates leak out of the formal programme and to set their own agendas. In our experience, this requires a careful balance: it is collegial to support colleagues by attending as much of the conference as possible (see more on 'being an audience' below), while at the same time you want to make the most of the opportunity to sketch out a possible research collaboration in person if you can (many a fantastic project has been devised on a conference napkin or in a breakout room session!). Certainly, this question of how present to be at the conference is a complex one and there is no right answer here. What we, the authors of this book, do is to try and maintain a high level of commitment to the conference, at the same time leaving space for the possibility that sometimes other things come up, including the possibility that the conference itself is disappointing, dull, or overwhelming and we need to hatch an escape plan! If we come away from a conference feeling stretched as well as intellectually reenergised, we tend to think that is time well spent.

3.3 Being an audience and asking questions

In a series of blog posts titled 'Survive and thrive at an academic conference', the Australian sociologist Raewyn Connell (2018) reminds us that the main thing that one does at an academic conference is to listen to others talk. Given that being an audience member occupies so much of our conferencing time, in this section we offer up some different ways to think about it. The first thing to note is that being an audience is partly about us. We might have objectives in attending a talk, perhaps to collect nuggets of useful information or to soak up some interesting ideas. However, being an audience is never *only* about us, it is also about others in the conference community (including other delegates and the presenters in sessions), and perhaps on an even wider level it's about being a participant in something bigger still: a citizen of our research field engaging with other citizens of that field. A lot of what other people need from audience members is for us to manage our ruder impulses. Here, we are thinking of those moments where academics might feel overly entitled to take up space (whether physical or temporal), or when a senior academic sits at the front of an early career researcher's session visibly buying their next airline ticket, or when someone answers their phone in a loud whisper and proceeds to have a conversation in the conference room, or when someone near the front gives into drowsiness and emits a long snore. While these might be more or less micro-moments of self-management, there's a theme here about exercising careful judgement in terms of how we show up for others, and as stewards who care about, and for, scholars and scholarship in our fields.

Larger conferences often cluster particular areas of work into 'streams'. Sometimes this works intellectually, and an audience might float along in the stream for much of the duration of the conference. At times, this feels less like an organic flow of ideas and more like an artificially constructed canal, for audience and presenters alike. Sometimes we can get a sense of whether presentations have been clumped or lumped early in the conference and plan any session-hopping accordingly. One thing to note with session-hopping is that it can also be logistically fraught. One of the reasons that session-hopping rarely works is because the timing of talks is seldom exact. This can lead to you traipsing across the venue to a session only to have missed a paper because another presenter hasn't shown up and the presentations have all been jiggled around to accommodate this. It's also challenging if presentations have been grouped together and there is a discussion to be held at the end of the session, and it can feel rather irritating to sit through a discussion of presentations you have not attended. Different conferences have differing norms about whether it is frowned upon or not to leave a streamed session. But it is fair to say that there is usually the possibility that some folks might get sniffy about delegates marauding through the conference promiscuously. It might be worthwhile experimenting with both the 'committed' and 'magpie' approaches to being an audience. It can be rewarding to stay in a stream that has been well-curated, and you may encounter things you might not have otherwise and end up with a good group of colleagues who stick around, so it can be a nice way of forming a community. On the other hand, if you are struggling to stay awake it might be better to abandon ship than to fall asleep in someone's session!

We've now discussed how you might make decisions about being an audience member, but there's also the small matter of what you should do with your body. For example, where do you sit? Any readers who are also teachers will be familiar with the experience of teaching a class of students who have all clustered at the back of a room. Raewyn Connell (2018) in the previously mentioned blog post describes this as the phenomenon of 'listeners clustered like frightened sheep near the door'. This doesn't tend to create the most dynamic environment for an exchange between scholars! We know it can feel difficult for newer researchers to take up space in the conference at all, let alone to sit at the front of the room near to the speaker. And sometimes, if we need to leave a session early, we may wish to sit close to an aisle or near the back. But in general, it is kind to a presenter to try to demonstrate engagement by where we sit.

Sticking with bodies, what do you do once you've taken your seat? Perhaps you unpack your pens and newly sharpened pencils, grab a notepad, or a computer and try to look vaguely intellectual. Maybe you self-consciously scroll on your phone, just willing the session to start, or perhaps you make eye contact and greet another audience member sitting nearby. But what to do once the session starts? Again, Raewyn Connell (2018) has some advice we think is well worth heeding, suggesting that researchers 'sit forward and listen *actively*'. Active listening may entail note taking and drawing doodles and mind maps, and engaging our brains in processing the information that is being shared. The mental processing that each person does depends to some degree on the field of inquiry they research in. But at a basic level you might be testing the claims of the presenter, the evidence they present, and the conclusions they have drawn based upon this evidence. Do you agree with the presenter? How does what they are presenting apply to, or affect what it is you are working on? Have you read anything saying something similar or different? Does anything that the presenter is saying minimise or silence any other perspectives? How about their citation politics—has the author only used cited authors from a particular gender or background in a way that might reproduce hegemonies in knowledge production? As you can see, there's lots to think about! Indeed, sometimes there is too much, and you might find yourself racing to catch up with a speaker presenting on a sub-sub-sub topic you have not encountered before. As an audience member, you might not only be thinking about *what* the presenter is saying but also *how* they are saying it. Savvy conference-goers may be noticing interesting ways of engaging an audience or a particular approach the speaker uses that works well. You might take notes on not only the content of the slides but also their design and arrangement. Equally, you might also pick up on presentational strategies that you wish to vigorously avoid.

At the end of a presentation or series of presentations, there is usually time for questions and even answers, although the length of time and arrangement of Q&A vary from conference to conference. What is the point of question time from the perspective of an audience member? Part of it might be about you and anything you don't understand or would like clarification about what the presenter has shared. For example, you might ask a specific question to the presenter that helps to draw out an aspect of the presentation that the presenter did not have time to expand upon, or ask clarification questions about aspects of a presentation that were not clear. Another function of Q&A is about wanting to share something with the presenter to help them go forward with their thinking—whether this is a theory, a reference, a methodological question, or so on. This is perhaps one of the most understandable functions of the Q&A and a generous audience member will think about how to ask questions that support the presenter to make further contributions to the discussion. Another function of Q&A on the part of an audience member might be about the epistemic claims that have been circulating in the room. Perhaps you think it is valuable for the presenter and the audience to hear a reaction or some alternative views to the thinking that has been presented, or maybe you want to offer public support and lift up what has already been shared. Our best advice is to observe other people who you think do it well. We both can think of colleagues in our field who can be counted on to ask highly perceptive questions to presenters. This rigorous engagement can be extremely generous, pushing thinking forward, stretching ideas around, and hopefully leading to more thoughtful knowledge production. A key message here, particularly for newer researchers, is that you don't have to be perfect. What matters is getting involved, asking the questions if you have them—doing one of *the* things that conferences allow researchers to do, which is to help each other to shape thinking in progress.

Perhaps you may be reluctant to speak up in question time because you don't want to be recognised as the bloviating question-asker who inevitably has 'more of a comment than a question' and takes the most long-winded way possible to get there. Certainly, it isn't good form to take up lots of space in the Q&A session by talking about your own research, or how you would have done things differently (it's not your research, after all, it's theirs). And many of us have groaned our way through a question time listening to questions that seem to function more to make the audience aware of the intelligence of the question-asker, or questions that would have been much better discussed over coffee at the end of the session. But we wonder if sometimes the criticism about poor question-asking leads to too many delegates remaining tight-lipped when they might, in fact, have questions that could open up new ideas for the presenter and audience alike. Given that question time is about negotiating over knowledge 'live', it is understandable that sometimes questions might be somewhat open-ended. While it is good to try and be as precise as possible, it is important to not let a desire for perfection get in the way of an important, if slightly unformed, thought. Rather than dismissing anything that does not end with a question mark, we argue that there are many different ways of engaging during the Q&A which can be edifying for the presenter.

As researchers, we need robust debate and even difficult questions which might contest what is being presented and identify flaws in thinking. But we can try to get clearer about intentions here—the goal is not to humiliate the other person or solely to demonstrate how smart the question-asker might be. As a steward of the field of knowledge, what do you think would improve the knowledge claims that are being presented?

Aiming to become a thoughtful audience member also calls for some reflexivity about one's own positionality. That is, trying to better understand one's positioning in relation to the wider social and political dynamics playing out at the gathering itself (and the world beyond the conference too). We find using an intersectional framework valuable for thinking with. An intersectional framework stipulates that individuals' lives are affected in different ways by the complex interplay between overlapping aspects of identity and different processes of privilege and marginalisation (Hancock, 2016; Hill Collins & Bilge, 2016). As audience members, we can try to attune ourselves to power relations that operate at conferences. Applying this intersectional framework to being an audience member can open up a multitude of questions (for more on this, see Chapter 6). For example, whose talks do you select to attend and why? Are there assumptions you make about presenters when you see their names and/or affiliations? If you reflect on them, do these assumptions make you feel uncomfortable about your own judgements? Who takes up the most airtime in discussion sessions, and why? Chewing on questions like this can help us become more thoughtful audiences at conferences.

3.4 Chairing a session

At some point in your conferencing career, you will likely be invited to serve as a 'session chair' or 'moderator' by conference organisers. In this section, we want to consider some advice and offer some provocations about acting in this role. Rather than tell you 'how to' in a prescriptive manner, we hope to instead flag up some different ways you might orient yourself to the possibilities that chairing opens up. Indeed, we think that the question of 'how do I chair a session?' can bring you into contact with your own values and ethics: Who am I here? What kind of chair does this session need? How can I add value? What are my scholarly values? How can I live out my scholarly values as I carry out this role?

Chairing at a conference generally means taking responsibility for managing the proceedings of a particular session. But just to make things confusing, the person or people who lead the organisation of the entire conference are also often called 'chairs' (e.g., "She is the chair of the conference this year"). In this section, focus on session chairs, and there is more information for conference chairs in Chapter 5 on 'Organising conferences'. At a basic level, the session chair is often responsible for: (1) ensuring the room or digital environment is set up, (2) introducing the session and speakers, (3) managing time, (4) staying alert and present, and (5) ensuring a fair and functional Q&A session. Additionally, sometimes the chair provides some concluding comments and then thanks the speakers and audience. In this section, we consider each of these key responsibilities in turn.

First, then, the chair ensures that the conference room (physical or virtual) is set up ready for the presentations to start. This includes arriving at the correct room on time—in a complex venue or new online platform, it can be a good idea to locate the room ahead of time. Arriving at the session early is helpful for checking that the equipment is working and that water is in place for the speakers—often these things will already be in place, but it is worth doing a final check if only for your peace of mind. As the chair, you can facilitate a calm start to the session by introducing yourself to the presenters (even by email beforehand) and can also confirm the session format so that everyone is aware (length of presentation, how the Q&A will work—including use of the chat window for online conferences). You may be in charge of making sure all the presentations are uploaded and that speakers know how to share their screen, mute their microphones and raise hands (for an online conference), and it is a good idea to find out the best way to ask for technical support if an issue arises. For online conferences, you may be asked to announce that the session will be recorded. There is something of a crisis handling role to chairing, so come prepared! The chair is also often the presence in the room that people will look to if there is background noise, or if the room is too hot or too cold, too light or too dark. For online chairing, it is vital to be as prepared as possible, as you need to be the stable presence in a sometimes volatile online environment, so it is wise to check your device is fully charged and that your technology and internet are functioning.

Second, it is your role as chair to introduce the session and the speakers. When introducing colleagues, it is important to be thoughtful and fair about each introduction. For example, audiences will likely pick up on overly lengthy and gushy introductions for some speakers and short and factual ones for others. It is advisable to keep the level of formality consistent across all speakers too, for instance in the use of titles or not, as this can give messages to the audience about who matters in the room. Formality is something that is important to think about more generally, given that academic conferences move around the world and different contexts anticipate varying levels of formality and usage of titles. When in doubt it is often safer to use a title than not when introducing someone (though getting the title wrong can be tricky). Prior to the session, it is important to learn how to pronounce speakers' names correctly. For some delegates, the experience of hearing their own name mispronounced time and again can contribute to feeling that this conference is not a space they belong to. If in doubt, approach someone tactfully via email or prior to the session and write down their name phonetically if necessary. Using the correct gendered pronouns for speakers and audience is another key practice for chairs to consider. If you make a mistake with a speaker's pronouns it is probably best to correct yourself as soon as possible and then move on swiftly. If you realise later that you accidentally misgendered someone, you might find a chance to discreetly apologise to them later. When referring to people you don't know personally in the audience, it may be advisable to avoid using gendered pronouns entirely. Some other key considerations include chairing from indigenous land and any protocols that might therefore be appropriate to follow. In Australia, for example, it is customary to acknowledge land/country and respect First Nations people as guardians and traditional owners of that land. It is best to check any guidance offered by conference organisers and/or traditional owners on how to honour local customs for welcome and gathering for both online and face-to-face conferences. Finally, when it comes to introductions: don't forget to welcome the audience and to introduce yourself and the institution you are affiliated with.

After setting up the space and undertaking introductions, another key role commonly taken by the session chair is to act as a timekeeper. The role of timekeeper involves two primary responsibilities: (1) to make sure the session ends on time, and (2) to make sure that time is fairly distributed. Delivering on both responsibilities is challenging for different reasons. One of these is that frequently presenters do not time their talks, often showing up with slides that are bulging at the seams. Another reason why keeping a session to time can be challenging is because of the power relations that are involved. Sometimes, rather junior chairs may be placed in the position of informing rather senior professors that their time is up! Despite the challenge, it is important that chairs ensure that everyone gets their fair turn, irrespective of their position in the academic food chain. In order to support this intention, at the beginning of the session, it can be helpful to state publicly how much time each speaker has and how you will be letting them know that their time is nearly up. If you find the timekeeping challenging, it can be useful to sketch out the timings out beforehand to help you keep track. One final thing to consider when keeping time: make sure the speaker can see and/or hear you clearly when you are giving them the message that the time is up.

Another key role of the chair is to stay present during the session. As the chair, you are often seated in full view of the entire room or, in an online conference, may be the only attendee with your camera on for the duration of the session. Audience members and presenters alike will notice if yawn your way through a presentation or seem to be answering emails. If you're live tweeting, the session you might decide to let the audience know that you are doing so, in case people think you are busy on your phone. Staying alert and present is also important because at times the chair may need to be flexible (e.g., redistributing time if a speaker fails to show up) or take on responsibility (e.g., having a question ready in case the

Q&A is quiet). Being attentive is important both for online and face-to-face conferences. For example, if gathering online you might be called upon to assist with people's differing levels of technology knowledge and interruptions that may arise as a result of working from home. You might have to improvise if suddenly the online conference system updates and throws half the audience out of the platform, or if an issue happens with a microphone and a presenter's voice develops a staccato electronic effect. Overall, staying attentive is really about being a supportive colleague and playing a necessary backstage role, so that the speakers of the session can rightly shine.

A final job for the chair is to manage the Q&A session. These can be the best bits of conferences and they are the spaces where a good chair can make a significant contribution to the conference itself. Sometimes a Q&A session opens up with a resounding silence, in which case the chair can start things off with a question while the attendees get thinking about their questions. On the other hand, multiple hands may shoot up at once, with more or less vigour and urgency—managing a queue system and also letting the audience know if there is no more time for further hands to go up are part of the chairing role. Sometimes chairs are given strict instructions for the Q&A, but at other times there may be scope to operate the space in a more pedagogical manner. One practice that can work well is the 'buzz', which is a short period of time after the presentation/s where audience members talk about their questions in pairs or small groups, and then the floor is opened up to questions for the speaker/s. This is operated by CHEER (Centre for Higher Education and Equity Research), University of Sussex, at their events, and has been strongly advocated by Critical Race and Indigenous Studies scholar

Eve Tuck in an influential (2019) Twitter thread, outlining the Indigenous Feminist approach that she uses to facilitate Q&A sessions. Another part of Eve Tuck's process is thinking carefully about who in the audience might be called upon to speak first (e.g., to prioritise those from social groups under-represented at a conference). Such a targeted approach to soliciting questions from the audience is arguably supported by scholarly evidence which suggests that, for example, if a man speaks first in Q&A, fewer women will contribute overall (King et al., 2018). Occasionally, the chair is required to step in to manage the session rather actively because of the behaviour of members of the session. As Critical Universities Studies scholar Tseen Khoo (2013) notes, to ensure that Q&A proceeds in a fair and respectful manner 'you may need to curtail showboaters, wafflers, and strangely vindictive and unhelpful people'. It is within the norms of chairing to interrupt a lengthy Q&A participant courteously to remind them to come to the point of their question, to seek help if you feel out of your depth, or even to end a session if the emotional dynamics become unmanageable.

We hope this section has given you an orientation to what chairing might involve. A key thing to remember is that we are all only human. A session chair might have been invited at the last minute, or given insufficient information on the workings of the session. And at the same time, the chair is also still juggling their own conference experience. The key thing about chairing is just to do our best.

3.5 Being a discussant

Aside from session chair, there is another role that one might be called on to perform at a conference: the role of discussant (sometimes also called a respondent). The basic definition of a discussant is someone who participates in a discussion, particularly a prearranged one. However, in practice, a discussant tends to have to come up with a set of ideas based on the paper or series of conference papers they have been invited to discuss, which then acts as an impromptu presentation in its own right. Often a discussant is deployed during a symposium or panel within a conference, where a series of papers share a common theme. Here, the discussant is tasked with giving an overall synthesis and commenting on how presenters have advanced knowledge in that area. While an exchange between participants may occur at the end, often the main thing a discussant does is give something of a monologue on the presentation/s they have witnessed. Sometimes the discussant will deliver this in a spontaneous manner, and at other times the presentation notes may be supplied in advance so the discussant can prepare a paper in advance about the papers they are due to witness! As you can see, there is a lot of variety in this role. However the discussant role is configured, it is likely to be intense. Much like the chair, the discussant needs to stay attentive to the papers they are listening to, as they are tasked with soaking up (or frantically collating) the information presented and responding to it publicly. In a previous post on our *Conference Inference* blog (Henderson & Burford, 2018), we have queried what the role of the discussant is all about. Is the purpose just to summarise the papers that were presented? Is it to capture the mood or responses of the room? To refer to all of the presentations or the major points made, to act as a linker and looper? Are there more cynical readings of the purpose of the role—is it about the discussant showcasing their own intelligence or opinions, or indeed showcasing their own work in the guise of responding to others' work? What is the content of a discussant's contribution, and how should they put it together?

There are some points to consider in answer to these questions, but it is also important to note that, as with many aspects of conferences, there is considerable variety in both conference organisers' expectations of the discussant, and the ways in which discussants enact the role. One general point is that discussants should avoid primarily using the opportunity to shine the spotlight on their own work. A second point is that there needs to be some balance to the discussant's talk; in terms of the amount of time and space given to each paper, as well as a balance in terms of praise and critique. The goal is to: recognise the achievements of individual presenters while, nonetheless, rigorously evaluating the contribution of their work (Barton, 2005). It can also be useful to thread through some reference to or discussion of other scholars' work if relevant, though maintaining the focus on the presentations at hand. Finally, it is a generous gesture to send your notes or comments across to the presenter/s after the session.

While the key steps of being a discussant are hopefully a little clearer, we want to end our discussion on the discussant with some further points we hope are valuable to consider. First, serving as a discussant is an act of generosity to the conference and to the field. On a personal level, it can be a good intellectual challenge, a new opportunity to meet new people, and have a detailed look at their work. Second, while preparation for being a discussant may be necessary or comforting, it can be impossible to be fully prepared for what happens when the knowledge is presented 'live'. The discussant may be surprised, or reoriented, and may need to revisit any script they have prepared in advance, based on how the knowledge lands in the room. There is also the question of how courageous a discussant might want to be. The discussant is in the position to offer a unique space to think about the unsaid, the assumed, the absent, the invisible, and invisibilised. The discussant can acknowledge the norms that have governed knowledge production of the day and can point to sparks and connections only recognisable from the heightened state of discussant thinking. However, it is possible too that a junior discussant feels they do not have enough authority to do anything too bold and walks a careful tightrope of fulfilling the objective of offering rigorous engagement, at the same time not stepping on senior toes.

3.6 Networking with the conference community, online and face-to-face

While there is much focus on the formal programme in discussions of conferences, much of the 'real work' of conferences is often done in, around, and instead of the formal sessions. In this section, we focus on conference networking, which is a key reason why researchers get together at in-person and online events. There are no fixed rules to follow when it comes to networking. Networking involves a complex mix of who you are, the folks present at the conference you're going to, the opportunities you have to connect, and the objectives and values you bring with you as you go about joining a community of scholars. Because networking is a contextualised and individual practice, we cannot provide a simple list of things to

Participating in a conference 67

do to become awesome at it. In what follows, we outline some areas to stimulate further thought about conference networking. You may wish to try out some suggestions if they feel like they would work for you, but you do not need to try them all. In our view, the goal with networking is to be a sociable and engaged version of yourself, not to transform yourself into someone else entirely.

Earlier in this chapter, we discussed the prior research that one can do before a conference even begins. This is also a starting point for networking. As you are reading through the conference booklet or website you will begin to notice the names of scholars who you would be interested to meet, and can start to develop a mental list. You might decide to follow them on available social media accounts (see Chapter 2) or even send them an email or a direct message to say hello and let them know that you are looking forward to seeing them present at the conference. It is not unusual for a researcher to contact another researcher to line up a meeting during one of the meal breaks at the conference or after the formalities conclude. Pre-planning some networking gives you the opportunity to prepare any questions or pitches for collaboration you might have for the person you are hoping to develop a collegial relationship with. Every relationship is inflected with its own characters and particularities, so there is some navigating to do here. For example, while there is nothing barring graduate students from reaching out to the conference keynote to suggest meeting over coffee, it is possible that their schedule might already be full. Networking online is another key feature of both online conferences and their in-person counterparts. Nowadays, the dining hall or atrium are not the only key zones to be participating in. Many researchers are also engaging on Twitter using the hashtag of the conference to share their reflections and get to know each other.

How about networking at the conference? What are some helpful strategies for this? First, it may be helpful to think of places where networking might more easily happen. For example, the queue for lunch or coffee is often a good place to strike up a conversation. The thing you are queuing for also gives you an innocuous topic to begin a conversation with. What this looks and sounds like will be different depending on your own authentic voice, but it could go something like: 'I'm so excited for a coffee!', 'Gosh I am starving', 'Wow! Look at those muffins!'. It doesn't need to be too deep or complicated! If you haven't had any luck in the meal or drinks queue, there are other places where people tend to be available for networking. Poster sessions or exhibits are similar kinds of spaces that give you an opportunity to appear alongside someone, and they offer you something to talk about. If you are out and about on the conference floor and looking for someone to talk to you could look for another delegate who is standing alone, possibly also looking for someone to talk to. What you might say to them again depends on what feels authentic for who you are and the values you are bringing forward. Perhaps you start with a compliment about their fantastic shoes, maybe you invite conversation about the keynote you've both just come from, perhaps you start with a casual introduction or a comment about the weather. There's no 'right' answer here, just what feels right for you.

There are countless strategies that might be employed when it comes to networking, and a good idea is to ask others how they do it or to try to pay close attention to others in action. For example, some people might head along to conferences with a mentor who might be able to facilitate connections. Others might aim to travel with a conference buddy, so they have some support when making connections with others. Some people carry business cards and try their best to remember to take them out of their luggage to give to others during networking sessions. Other people might take a different role, preferring to be the connector who plays the role of introducing people who do not know each other yet. While there are some things that you can practice in advance, including your 'elevator pitch' (or short description of your research), much networking is more of a 'being' than a 'doing', and simply hoping to follow a recipe or algorithm often doesn't work for building sustaining relationships.

3.7 Conference embodiment: Eating, drinking, and more!

Conferences can facilitate many fleshy joys: hugs with old friends, the enlivening disorientation of being in new places, opportunities for rich intellectual stimulation, and the special feeling of becoming a part of an academic community, among others. And yet conferences, in all their embodied glory, also facilitate opportunities for disconnection, alienation, jealousies, exhaustion, and the sheer awkwardness of being a human person in a new place and/or time zone. They can be tough events, where delegates navigate sometimes complex social, political, and intellectual scenes. Academic conferences are also events where the folk who we often know in our reading and writing as '(Surname, date)' become corporeal creatures. These creatures might be wonderful, generous, and kind. And yet in their all-too-human form they might also be monsters who bump into us, spill their tea, and rub it into the carpet, dither in the lunch queue, talk too long or too loudly, amid a wide array of other naughty things. If we are honest with ourselves, we might even find that we are these monsters sometimes too. The visceral nature of conferences can make them awkward spaces to inhabit, particularly for those of us who find that awkwardness easily finds us.

In this section, we zoom in to focus on a side of conferencing which we are calling conference embodiment, which has become a regular feature of the *Conference Inference* blog (https://conferenceinference.wordpress.com/category/bodies-in-places/). We will start with food, a topic at the centre of much chatter for conference organisers and delegates alike. One of the facts of most in-person conferences is that they free delegates, momentarily at least, from the obligation of reproductive labour (cooking, cleaning, dishwashing, etc.) to harness their energy towards knowledge production. Free from providing for their own meals, it is hoped that conference delegates can devote time to networking and knowledge production. Often much energy and forethought has gone into planning meals for delegates, and being nourished by good food at the conference can be one of the highlights of the event. Indeed, when interviewing academics for a cultural history project on the International Academic Identities Conference, Jamie found that some interviewees had much clearer memories of what they ate for lunch than what they presented at the event!

However, conference meals are also complex for many reasons. First, it is important to remember that while delegates might be freed from domestic work for the duration of the conference this does not mean that the work itself disappears. There is often a whole team

Participating in a conference 71

of caterers and wait staff who care for delegates, and it is worth contemplating how to make life easier for those who are looking after you. There are all kind of complexities that may arise with conference food. The food you are served may not be the kind of food you are used to. Perhaps you have travelled to a conference in another country, and are being served a local delicacy that does not whet your appetite. Perhaps you are being met by tray after tray of cold sandwiches, when you were anticipating a hot meal. Perhaps you have dietary requirements, which you have flagged to organisers, but the food marked for you is descended upon by droves of hungry delegates. Maybe the organisers have under-catered and there are delegates who are left hungry or with something less than appealing. Because conference meals are rife with risks of all kinds, it can be worthwhile to carry some reliable snacks with you just in case.

Another of the peculiar things about conferences is that the social occasions that they generate often involve socialising while eating. Not only this, but often one is doing this while standing for lengthy periods in professional attire, which one is trying desperately not to spill food onto. This is a challenging situation where spills and stains are even more likely to occur than usual. One might plan for this by bringing a spare shirt or simply embracing the possibility that mess might occur!

In addition to packing a spare shirt, dancing shoes can come in useful! Yes, some conferences do have their own disco. When we have spoken to friends of the existence of such dancing at higher education conferences they often react with surprise or disdain. What? Ugh. Dancing professors? It's as if the movement of the academic body is in some way embarrassing, as if academics should properly be talking heads at the front of the room rather than embodied persons jiggling and wiggling in the semi-darkness. Yet typing 'conference disco' into an internet search reveals that a diverse array of fields maintain these rituals. It is, of course, up to you how much you wish to participate in them, but it can be a nice chance to let your hair down.

3.8 Actions post-conference

What might it mean to finish a conference well, and what follow-up activities might delegates undertake post-conference? Depending on how your networking went at the conference you might now have a short or long list of names, a pocketful of business cards, a notepad containing social media accounts or email addresses that you want to sit down and sift through. Taking some time to cement the contacts that you have made is well worth the effort. While it is possible that a friendship might emerge if you run into a colleague sometime down the line, it is often the follow-through of emailing contacts, following on social media like LinkedIn or Twitter, and sending direct messages that gives the connections you have made at the conference a chance to flourish. You might also want to schedule further meetings (e.g., via video conference) to finish any conversations that you felt were rushed or unfinished. Often once we get home after a conference there are many things that scream for our immediate attention, and it can be challenging to prioritise writing a note to a colleague. Even if a few weeks have passed by it can still be a good idea to send a note to establish the connection.

It's not only following up with key contacts at the conference that matters, hopefully there has been some learning happening too. It is worth taking some time to make sense of all the new ideas and information that you have been exposed to. You might do this on the plane, train, or bus ride home if you have been to a conference in person, or schedule some time in your diary to draw out any key insights. Once you have done some of this processing for yourself, you might consider sharing it with others. If you work as part of a lab group or research team, you could offer to give a lunchtime presentation where you bring back relevant work from the conference to share with others. If you are working in a more solo kind of way, perhaps you might spend some time in a supervision meeting debriefing with your supervisor/s about key ideas that have emerged, or offer to give a talk in your department for any other colleagues who may be interested. There are also ways of sharing conference learning via social media or blogging. You could identify key takeaways and create a Twitter thread so that others who were not a part of the conference can engage with the ideas that have been floating around there. Or perhaps you could write a post for your own blog or contribute a guest post for a blog that your institution or a member of your discipline curates. Undertaking either of these actions can be good for you, giving you an opportunity to puzzle over the conference and draw out what you've learned, and it can also be a generous thing to do for others in your field who didn't have access to the event itself.

Finally, there is rest and caring for your body, which might have been eating new kinds of foods, meeting new people, in new places, and staying up well past your normal bedtime. After a conference, it can be a good idea to plan to have some time off work. If you have travelled to another location for a conference, you could to take some time to explore the location you have come a long way to visit. It can also be valuable to schedule some time off when you get back to your home location too. If you have the possibility, giving yourself space to recover from jetlag or the weariness of travel, in addition to sorting out any disruptions to care and household functionings that have occurred in your absence, could be a worthwhile thing to do.

***

In this chapter, we have set out some key areas to contemplate when it comes to taking part in a conference, and have offered some provocations to help you imagine what participating might look like. If there's one message to take away from this chapter, it is this: be curious and thoughtful about how you might be at conferences, but don't try and force yourself into being someone else. We don't all have to aspire to slickness or live up to all the advice that 'how to' websites offer us. What a boring conference that would be! While conferences have norms and conventions that they operate by, as participants in the conference we also have some role in shaping the kind of conference we want to be a part of. Another key message from this chapter is that participating in conferences can be unpredictable, and one's experience of them can shift rapidly. Even highly experienced conference-goers may not glide serenely through the venue. Whatever your level of experience, the complex social work of being human in the company of professional others whom we want to think well of us is not to be underestimated. So let's not overthink mix-ups and muddles, spilt milk, and lengthy conversations about the weather. It's all part of the experience.

3.9 Further resources: Participating in a conference

- Edwards, D., Foley, C., & Malone, C. (2017). *The Power of Conferences: Stories of serendipity, innovation and driving social change*. Sydney: University of Technology Sydney ePress.
- Henderson, E. F. (2019a). Academics in two places at once: (not) managing caring responsibilities at conferences. In R. Finkel, B. Sharp, & M. Sweeney (Eds.), *Accessibility, Inclusion, and Diversity in Critical Event Studies* (pp. 218–229). London; New York, NY: Routledge.
- Hinsley, A., Sutherland, W. J., & Johnston, A. (2017). Men ask more questions than women at a scientific conference. *PLoS One, 12*(10), e0185534. doi:10.1371/journal.pone.0185534
- Kenway, J., Epstein, D., & Boden, R. (2005). *Building networks*. London: Sage.
- King, L., Mackenzie, L., Tadaki, M., Cannon, S., McFarlane, K., Reid, D., & Koppes, M. (2018). Diversity in geoscience: Participation, behaviour, and the division of scientific labour at a Canadian geoscience conference. *Facets, 3*, 415–440. doi:10.1139/facets-2017-0111
- Nicolazzo, Z., & Jourian, T. J. (2020). 'I'm looking for people who want to do disruption work': Trans* academics and power discourses in academic conferences. *Gender and Education, 32*(1), 56–69. doi:10.1080/09540253.2019.1633461
- Yoo, H., & Wilson, E. (2020). 'More than a travel companion': Accompanying partners' experiences of conference attendance. *Gender and Education, 32*(1), 43–55. doi:10.1080/09540253.2019.1688259

References

Barton, K. C. (2005). Advancing the conversation: The roles of discussants, session chairs, and audience members at AERA's annual meeting. *Educational Researcher, 34*(9), 24–28. doi:10.3102/0013189X034009024

Connell, R. (2018, June). Survive and thrive 3: How to give a conference paper. [Blog post]. *Raewyn Connell*. Available: http://www.raewynconnell.net/2018/06/survive-thrive-3-how-to-give-conference.html (last accessed 25 January 2022).

Edwards, D., Foley, C., & Malone, C. (2017). *The Power of Conferences: Stories of serendipity, innovation and driving social change*. Sydney: University of Technology Sydney ePress.

Hancock, A-M. (2016). *Intersectionality: An intellectual history*. New York: Oxford University Press.

Henderson, E. F. (2019). Academics in two places at once: (Not) managing caring responsibilities at conferences. In R. Finkel, B. Sharp, & M. Sweeney (Eds.), *Accessibility, Inclusion, and Diversity in Critical Event Studies* (pp. 218–229). London; New York: Routledge.

Henderson, E. F. & Burford, J. (2018, 19 November). Discussing the discussant—A Queer-ish role? [Blog post]. Conference inference: Blogging the world of conferences. Available: https://conferenceinference.wordpress.com/2018/11/19/discussing-the-discussant-a-queer-ish-role/ (last accessed 08 February 2022).

Hill Collins, P., & Bilge, S. (2016). *Intersectionality*. Cambridge: Polity Press.

Hinsley, A., Sutherland, W. J., & Johnston, A. (2017). Men ask more questions than women at a scientific conference. *PLoS One, 12*(10), e0185534. doi:10.1371/journal.pone.0185534

Kenway, J., Epstein, D., & Boden, R. (2005). *Building networks*. London: SAGE.

Khoo, T. (2013, 15 October). How to chair. [Blog post]. *Research Whisperer.* Available: https://researchwhisperer.org/2013/10/15/how-to-chair/ (06 February 2022).

King, L., Mackenzie, L., Tadaki, M., Cannon, S., McFarlane, K., Reid, D., & Koppes, M. (2018). Diversity in geoscience: Participation, behaviour, and the division of scientific labour at a Canadian geoscience conference. *Facets, 3*, 415–440. doi:10.1139/facets-2017–0111

Nicolazzo, Z., & Jourian, T. J. (2020). 'I'm looking for people who want to do disruption work': Trans* academics and power discourses in academic conferences. *Gender and Education, 32*(1), 56–69. doi:10.1080/09540253.2019.1633461

Tuck, E. [@tuckeve] (2019, June 20). *I was just asked by a colleague how I facilitate Q & A sessions—I guess the word is out that I* [Tweet]. Twitter. https://twitter.com/tuckeve/status/1141501422611128320?lang=en-GB

Yoo, H., & Wilson, E. (2020). 'More than a travel companion': Accompanying partners' experiences of conference attendance. *Gender and Education, 32*(1), 43–55. doi:10.1080/09540253.2019.1688259

4 Presenting at conferences

Figure 4.1 'No input' by Rhiannon Nichols

4.1 Introducing conference presenting

Presenting at conferences is one of the most important tools researchers have to communicate their ideas. The frequency, types of conference, and locations covered

DOI: 10.4324/9781003144885-4

may vary widely, but there is usually some expectation that academic work will be presented to others. This expectation translates into some formalised expectations, for instance in recruitment criteria (often for early career positions where an established publication record may not be expected yet) and in academic promotion criteria. The expectation is also there informally, reproduced by peers and colleagues and on social media. Often funding to attend conferences is predicated on giving a presentation. So, clearly presenting is a practice that counts for researchers. But when it comes to navigating the process of proposing, preparing, and giving a presentation at a conference, there are many choices and (often unspoken) norms which can be bewildering for new and indeed experienced presenters. The presence of these unspoken norms also means that doing something creative or different and indeed challenging the norms can feel daunting. This chapter covers preparing an abstract for a conference presentation, choosing a presentation type (e.g., poster, workshop, round table), preparing to present, the Q&A session, and the post-presentation period. As such, the chapter offers an overarching view of the process of presenting at a conference, both from a practical point of view and by raising some critical issues for presenters to consider. We hope it allows readers to learn the 'rules' as well as hopefully question, critique, and even resist these rules.

4.2 Producing an abstract

Abstracts are often mentioned but rarely discussed and can therefore be something of a mystery to conference newcomers. Conference abstracts are short texts that are generally submitted before the conference as part of the selection process and which then go on to serve multiple purposes during and beyond the lifetime of the conference. Typically, abstracts include the title of the presentation and between 200 and 500 words on what will be covered. Sometimes an abstract is the only text which is required when proposing a presentation to a conference; for other conferences, the abstract is accompanied by a written paper which may range from 1,000 words to a full-length journal-style paper (paper length varies by discipline, but this could be 7,000 words or more). In the first case, the abstract is particularly important as it is the only basis for the conference organisers to decide who will present at the conference and who may not be accepted to present. In the second case, the importance of the abstract recedes slightly as the work can be fleshed out in the fuller paper. But the abstract is still very important as conference organisers will often conduct an initial reviewing sweep of the abstracts to determine which papers will go through to full review. If the paper's relevance to the conference or the quality of the abstract does not meet the required standards, this can lead to a 'desk reject' of the paper before the full paper is even taken into consideration. Though the abstract is only a short text, its importance is therefore rather inflated—and crafting a 'good' abstract is an art in itself (Burford & Henderson, 2020).

A conference abstract is charged with different tasks. It needs to meet the requirements of various audiences—some of whom have competing priorities. For instance, the abstract needs to meet the expectations of the conference organisers. This may include demonstrating relevance to the theme and/or disciplinary orientation of the conference; adhering to any requirements in the call for papers (e.g., length, style, elements to include); clearly indicating that the work will be ready in time to present at the conference; showing evidence of the competence and expertise of the author. A competing priority is that the abstract is often included in the conference programme or a supplementary booklet, and then this small piece of text goes on to serve as the principal way in which other attendees decide to come along to the presentation—or not. It is worth noting that, while sometimes presenters may be allowed to edit their abstract before wider distribution, this varies from conference to conference. A diligently produced abstract may meet all the organisers' needs but have zero appeal for other conference attendees. The abstract, and indeed the title of the presentation, therefore need to include some appeal—why would attendees choose to come along to this paper, rather than the others running at the same time—or rather than skipping the session to have a chat or catch up on email? The appeal needs to be balanced with the organisers' requirements—too much excitement and the organisers may not take the abstract seriously. Much of this is about tuning into the vibe of the conference: reading the web information carefully, looking at information and abstracts (if available) from previous versions of the conference, asking for advice from colleagues and mentors. The abstract will also help conference organisers to timetable the presentation slot for the paper, and here again, a clear and direct message about why the paper will be attractive to attendees is helpful in securing a primetime slot on the programme. Finally, the abstract will remain as part of the conference archive – increasingly conference abstracts can be located on conference websites as a permanent and accessible archive of the conference.

Therefore, some consideration to this longevity is worthwhile, particularly in terms of making confrontational/controversial comments about other researchers' work in the abstract ….

Having thought about the purpose and audience of the abstract, it may feel quite impossible to actually sit down and write one of these tiny yet important texts. Most guides to producing an abstract do not start with all this, but it is our view that understanding this contextual information helps abstract authors to understand why writing such a short text can feel so challenging—and to think beyond the technical task of representing a whole project in just a few words. Thinking about size and scope is key so you don't promise things you can't deliver or spend too much time talking about a tiny thing.

Moving on now to thinking about how to craft an abstract, it is important to remember that the abstract is representing two things: (i) the presentation, and (ii) the wider project that the presentation is nestled within. The second thing may be less relevant if the presentation is not drawing on a wider project. However, most presentations are based on a wider project, whether this be a doctoral thesis, a book project, a small- or large-funded research project. The conference abstract is *not* an abstract for the project as a whole—this is a mistake often made by novice abstract writers. It is often not possible to present a whole project in 15–20 minutes, and the abstract needs to indicate the specific focus of the presentation. An abstract therefore needs to indicate that the presentation is drawing on a wider project, with some brief information about this, but the presentation—its topic, structure, argument—is the focus of the abstract. This also helps to provide a foundation for planning the presentation nearer the time we will give it—a generous gift to our future selves! The craft of writing a conference abstract relies on balance: a balance of information given about, for example, our topic/field, context, methodology, theory, the overall project, specific presentation topic, presentation structure, argument, findings/main points to be made. Sometimes we are deep in a particular aspect of our work—perhaps we are submitting an abstract at the time of working on the theoretical framework or a chapter about the research context—and this can pervade the abstract, to the detriment of the other important aspects. Writing a conference abstract is actually a useful exercise to step back from the current focus in order to gain some perspective on the whole endeavour, thinking ahead to the point in time where the presentation will be given.

Abstracts are multi-faceted, multi-purpose texts, which also signal something about their authors as researchers. Writing them can be painful and uncomfortable, but also very useful in terms of taking stock of the research narrative we are constructing about our work—and about ourselves. Seeking feedback from peers and mentors is often valuable in the early days, as no amount of advice can replace the necessary process of gaining experience by writing abstracts for different types of conferences.

4.3 Choosing a type of presentation

With some conferences, there is no choice element; there is only one option available to 'regular' (i.e., not keynote) attendees, namely, to give an oral presentation for a set length of time (e.g., 15 minutes). For other conferences, there may be any number of choices to make, and navigating this terrain can be rather confusing. One option open to prospective presenters is to choose a shorter or longer presentation slot. This may be presented in terms of work in progress versus complete work, or just left open for choice. The choice of presentation length, where it is offered, is imbued with power relations. There are unwritten assumptions around the choice of shorter slots for more junior researchers. A research study has also shown that there is a gendered aspect to this choice, with more men opting for the longer presentation slots (Jones et al., 2014). There is no harm in opting for the shorter slots for reasons of confidence or preparedness. However, it is always worth remembering that conference organisers can decide to move a presentation from a longer slot to a shorter slot but will rarely move a presentation from a shorter slot to a longer one. It may be worth taking the risk and submitting for a longer slot.

Other choices may include:

- poster and/or poster presentation
- workshop
- round table
- panel/symposium

Conferences offering a poster option may include simply displaying the poster in a physical space or an online 'room' (where a researcher can even send a poster without attending the conference), or a range of options from a scheduled formal slot to present the poster, to a networking session where poster authors stand in front of their posters during a break between oral presentations or join an online poster session to present the poster as part of a break. Submitting a poster often still involves submitting an abstract, which is a somewhat different task to writing an abstract for an oral presentation, as the abstract becomes a textual account of the poster. The poster is more likely to display a summarised depiction of the project as a whole, so the abstract would then follow suit. In some fields, giving a poster presentation is often thought of as a way of early career researchers starting their conference careers, especially as it may be easier to be accepted to a poster slot than an oral presentation in heavily oversubscribed association conferences. However, there is a limitation as poster presentations may have less impact than other types of presentations if they are stuffed into an over-packed hall or online gallery with little time for people to read them. As with all these judgements, asking your supervisors and peers for their input can be valuable as can reading resources created by poster enthusiasts (see further resources at the end of the chapter).

Offering a workshop is a different kind of endeavour, and it is important to think carefully before selecting this option. Workshops have a specific purpose: to engage participants in participatory, interactive learning at the conference. Before proposing a workshop, a prospective workshop facilitator needs to think carefully about the workshop's purpose. Workshops have the potential to get participants thinking in different ways about things through doing things differently—and the best kinds of workshops that we have attended have been facilitated by people who are genuinely interested in providing a different conference experience for attendees. Proposing a workshop is certainly not taking the easy option. Workshop proposals may be scrutinised more carefully than other abstract submissions, as they tend to be allotted longer programme slots and therefore must demonstrate care of thought, so it may actually be harder to get a workshop accepted. Planning a workshop in advance is also important—again this is not an easy option as, although much of the 'input' may be from participants, curating the space and considering the pedagogy are extremely important. We have both attended deeply frustrating workshops which are not 'real' workshops— for instance, a facilitator or facilitating group who give a standard academic presentation and then open up for discussion; a question or set of questions posed to the audience and then resounding silence while the audience is supposed to fill the rest of the unstructured time with their reflections. At the other end of the frustration is where a facilitator has been too ambitious and cannot make a complex set of materials or activities fit within the time slot and venue. Some of the most exciting conference activities we have attended (and sometimes facilitated) have been workshops, but this option should be selected with caution and approached thoughtfully as a space for alternative ways of engaging in conference knowledge production.

Round tables, panels, and symposia are names for similar conference presentation formats—and they are sometimes used interchangeably, or other terms are used instead. It is advisable to check the call for papers carefully as to what is expected for these formats, as this can vary widely, and contact the conference organisers if anything is unclear. What unites these types of presentations is that they are all oral presentations, and all of them involve multiple speakers who are in some way giving an individual presentation within a group format. The differences occur in terms of what is expected in advance as well as what happens on the day. In the most formal version of this type of presentation, sometimes known as a symposium (within a conference as opposed to a standalone symposium event), a symposium convenor collects a set of approximately 3–5 presenters around a particular theme. To propose this, the convenor may be asked to submit an abstract with the rationale for the symposium as a whole; paper authors then may also be asked to submit abstracts for their papers, which are reviewed separately. On the day, the symposium may take the form of separate paper presentations, with a short Q&A after each one and/or a longer discussion after all the papers. There may also be a discussant or respondent whose role is to give an initial synthesis of and commentary on the papers to stimulate discussion (for more information on being a discussant, see Chapter 3). A less formal version, sometimes known as a round table, may involve just one abstract submission from the round table convenor, explaining the rationale for the round table and indicating the perspectives of the speakers. This format normally involves shorter initial presentations from the roundtable participants, perhaps taking the form of a five-minute provocation without slides, which then leads into a discussion between the round table participants and the audience. A round table is suitable for a debate including different perspectives—and is sometimes less suitable if the presenters need to gain official evidence of giving a formal presentation for career and/or funding purposes, so it is best to check with your funder about this. While proposing these group presentations may appear to be an option for more senior/confident researchers and may also appear daunting due to the need to corral various speakers into providing information and registration, it can also be very worthwhile engaging in these collective endeavours. It gives a ready-made group to hang out with at the conference and can lead to highly engaging debate and discussion. Choosing this option can also result in or contribute to the formation of a research community, perhaps even leading to collaborative projects and publications in the future. Indeed, participating in one such symposium in 2014 is what led to us becoming friends and eventually to writing this book! While in some disciplines participating in these formats holds significant prestige or is seen as equivalent to a 'presentation slot', in other fields these formats are sometimes what one is assigned if a proposal is judged to be below the quality required for a full presentation slot. So, as with all conference decisions we raise in this book, it is valuable to seek advice from colleagues in your own discipline.

A starting point to get orientated in relation to these choices is to think about (i) what the purpose of the presentation is for the wider knowledge project and (ii) who we are in relation to the conference and what wider purpose the presentation serves in terms of, for example, career development and network formation.

In relation to the first point, there may be various purposes for the knowledge project: to practice presenting the work in order to gain a more cogent view of the project (oral/poster presentation); to gain feedback from a specialist or more generalist audience (oral/poster presentation); to try out ideas in a different disciplinary space (oral/poster presentation/workshop); to understand a topic in more detail through a participatory/interactive mode (workshop/round table); to prepare for a project proposal, a joint publication or edited collection (round table/symposium).

The second point includes thinking about comfort and discomfort, as well as aspiration. Is this an unfamiliar space in terms of institution or association, geographical context, or disciplinary area? In which case selecting a 'safer' presentation mode might be a good option, such as a shorter oral presentation or a poster. Is this a more familiar space? In which case opting for a 'statement' presentation mode may be worthwhile—for example, facilitating a workshop or convening a round table or panel/symposium. There is no harm in testing the water with a 'safer' option, and getting a feel of conference rules often involves going along with the rules before being able to question the norms. Breaking the rules can involve, for example, requesting a different kind of presentation to those available in the call for papers, by approaching the organisers and asking them to consider a different option—this could take the form of a performance or exhibition. Another way of doing this is to submit an abstract for a type of presentation that is offered in the call for papers and then subverting the norms on the day— perhaps by giving a presentation in the form of a song and dance or bringing in workshop elements. Subversion usually has a politicised motivation—such as confronting the rigid norms of academic knowledge production from a feminist perspective (as with the FAAB group—'Feminists Against Academic Bollocks'). The potential for subversion to work is, however, also based on existing academic hierarchies, where it may be easier to 'get away with it' for more senior academics and/or academics located in the knowledge production powerhouses of the Global North. Spaces of experimentation and subversion may be open to less privileged, early career academics via mass organising, or indeed by seeking these spaces in, for example, conferences for doctoral and/or early career researchers, or by taking the reins and organising a conference.

4.4 Preparing to present

Preparing for presentations is one of those areas of conferencing—like agonising over crafting an abstract (see Section 4.2)—which is somewhat obfuscated in academia. Often these aspects of academia are hidden from sight because anxiety and shame are attached to them, including for the most seasoned presenters. Preparation is also a highly personal process, as the type of preparation needed depends on what happens to each individual when they open their mouth to present to a group of people, or to a computer screen with a hidden set of attendees. More preparation is needed for new presenters, or for any presenters if the presentation is on new work (it doesn't necessarily get easier), or in a second or third (or fourth …) language. More preparation may also be needed for presenters who are shy or who have less experience of public speaking or speaking out in professional contexts. This section focuses on preparing for an oral presentation, whether this is a standard oral presentation, a poster presentation, or a contribution to a symposium. Other presentation formats (Section 4.3) demand further preparation: a face-to-face poster presentation requires ensuring the poster is printed, arrives in one piece, and is correctly displayed; a workshop necessitates planning and consideration of materials; a group presentation, such as a symposium or round table, requires that the convenor communicates all requirements to the other members of the group.

Preparation for an oral presentation may take the form of writing out the entire paper, word for word, in order to deliver it at the conference. In some disciplines, often within the Humanities, this is a norm and would be expected. The advantages of writing out the full paper are numerous: the presenter's (potentially jetlagged) brain does not have to function spontaneously on the day; complex ideas can be reliably conveyed; the text can be converted easily into a publication. There are, however, disadvantages: listening to a pre-written paper is often difficult to sustain, especially if the delivery is not engaging; if the paper is too long it is difficult to adapt on the spot, with whole sections being skipped and a lot of flustered page flipping occurring; if there is a last-minute change to the length of the presentation slot, again the paper is less adaptable in this circumstance. It is important to find out what the disciplinary expectations are from mentors and potentially from conference organisers.

Instead of writing out the paper, some presenters take more or less detailed notes that they use to structure the presentation. This can involve writing down the sections, the main points, the timings—and varying amounts of information that is uttered verbatim or adapted on the day. Notes may be on a separate piece of paper or screen—in which case, if using a visual form of presentation as well, it is important to consider and rehearse how the notes and slides interact, and how many actions will be asked of the potentially flustered presenting versions of ourselves. Are we asking ourselves to turn pages and move slides on at the same time? Is this feasible? On the other hand, notes may be included in the 'notes' function of software such as PowerPoint. This works well, so long as the flustered presenter is absolutely sure that they can operate the computer on the day to be able to show the slides and also to see the notes, without showing the notes to the audience. Sometimes we are capable of surprisingly little while we are presenting! Another option is to include all the necessary information on the slides. This does not necessarily mean overloading the slides, but rather ensuring that all prompts are included on the slides. Doing this means that we are trusting ourselves to pick up on these cues on the day—and a serious rehearsal is advisable for this strategy.

Regardless of the extent to which you decide to write out the presentation beforehand, you will need to decide how to structure the presentation. There are different schools of thought on this which may have their own disciplinary inflections. One way of structuring a presentation is referred to as 'IMRAD', that is, Introduction, Methods, Results, Discussion, and Conclusion. This is of course most relevant to presentations that are reporting on empirical work, as opposed to theoretical papers. An alternative format is proposed by Raewyn Connell (2018), who suggests beginning in a brief manner with the problem, stating the main finding, then presenting the reasoning that explains how the presenter reached the finding (including information on the methodology), and then discussing the relevance or significance of the work, including situating the work within the relevant literature. Whichever structure you choose, you can also play within the format, adapting the emphasis of the sections to suit the specific presentation in question.

Rehearsing a presentation before giving it is highly recommended for novice presenters. Keeping to time is essential, and many presentations are ruined because they are too long and are then rushed and truncated in a stressful battle with the clock and the chair or moderator of the session. Making the time to rehearse is well worth the effort—even if it is in an airport or before breakfast, as being able to confidently deliver a presentation makes for a much more positive conference experience overall and means that the purpose/s of presenting (Section 4.3) are more likely to come to fruition. It also means that a presenter can focus on 'being there' in the other sessions of the conference with the assurance that they are well prepared for their session. Under-preparation can colour the rest of a conference and result in unnecessary stress and heartache.

An added aspect of preparation for those giving online presentations or in-person presentations involving technology is to rehearse the technological processes beforehand.

Finally, preparing also includes preparing for others to engage with your presentation. This means practicing a projecting voice, checking pronunciation if presenting in another language, but it also means taking into consideration how to make the presentation as accessible as possible. With a conference, it is more difficult than in the workplace or a classroom to establish which accessibility adjustments may be needed, as often a presenter has no idea who will be attending the presentation. Some tasks can be incorporated into the conference preparation to-do list which at least cover some potential accessibility issues—and which may also make the presentation more accessible for all. For instance, if slides are used, bringing a couple of copies of the slides in large print and/or on pale-yellow paper and indicating that these are near the door ensures that visually impaired and ASD (Autism Spectrum Disorder) audience members will be able to more comfortably access the slides. Using a pale-yellow backing for the slides has the same effect and ensuring that the font size is not below size 24 is helpful. If you are presenting online, you might begin by describing yourself and the context you are speaking from for the benefit of anyone else present who may have a visual impairment.

4.5 Working with technology and social media

Increasingly, giving a presentation no longer involves simply speaking to a live audience with no technological involvement. Involving technology in presentations ranges from showing PowerPoint slides to engaging in more complex interactive arrangements—and includes giving presentations in virtual environments. Deciding how to use technology involves a number of different thought processes. A major factor in these decisions is the availability of facilities in the venue (if conferencing in person) that can support any plans to use more sophisticated technology. While most venues support the projection of slides onto a screen, there are even risks here as sometimes the projector is incompatible with a presenter's personal laptop (it may be useful to travel with a VGA and HDMI projector adaptor or check if you can borrow these for a conference), there may be an issue with the file (always wise to come accompanied with a pdf version) and there may also be power outages, which are more or less common depending on the conference context. It is always worth thinking about how the presentation could still be delivered with complete technology failure, as it happens more often than one might expect! Risk-averse planning is necessary, but this does not mean that we should plan not to use technology at all—rather, presenters need to be flexible and consider fallback options.

The use of visual and audiovisual aids to accompany presentations is a fraught area of discussion, and as discussed in Section 4.4 there are disciplinary norms that influence these decisions. For some disciplinary areas, presenting with projected slides is an expectation, while in others reading out a scripted paper is the norm. In our view, it is important to look beyond the idea that there is a 'good' way of presenting. Many 'how to' guides on presentations settle on 'good' use of slides, advising presenters to not use them, or to include a certain amount of information—no more, no less. This is a rather universalising view, which assumes that all presentations are given in the same conditions. Yes, there are certainly some uses of slides that may be less advisable—for instance writing the entire presentation out and displaying it on slides in tiny font. Rather than adhering to universal norms about the use of slides, it is perhaps more sensible for the individual presenter to think about what would help them to give the best version of the presentation, taking into account the context where the presentation will be delivered and the potential audience. More information on slides is useful for presenters who are less confident about the language they will be presenting in, for instance. If giving a presentation about a phenomenon or context that is unfamiliar to the audience, showing images or other visual information can be helpful. If giving a presentation to a multilingual audience who may struggle to keep up, including plenty of clear information on slides is also useful. Aside from using PowerPoint slides as a visual aid, there are other programmes such as Prezi which allow for a more interactive style of presentation, where the presentation zooms in and out of different information. This can cause motion sickness though, so balancing the interactivity of the on-screen motion with its usefulness is worth considering. Some presenters use the slides as a form of wallpaper, including a series of images that rotate—again it is worth considering how to balance the focus of the audience versus their distraction.

Many presenters use audio and/or visual materials in their presentations. This is where the technology risk factor is increased, as the potential for incompatibility with these types of files and the malfunction of the sound equipment is relatively common. Examples of this use of technology include showing clips from projects that have included making a short film or playing audio clips of data (with permission from participants) or showing a cultural phenomenon via a video clip. Here, the best things to do are to (a) check with organisers that the platform/programme you are using for the clip is compatible with the conference technology, and (b) test the clip at the beginning of the conference so you can make a backup plan if needed. It is a good idea to have a backup plan regardless, given how fickle technology can be, as many a presentation slot has been wasted—with the result that the presentation (or the following presentation at times) is truncated—waiting for the technology manager to arrive. Backup options include a printed version of the slides/paper/notes, deciding how to fill the time or describe the film clip if the audiovisual technology fails, bringing copies, for example on an USB stick that do not require the internet to download. The risk also applies with online presentations—sometimes video clips do not play so that the audience can hear them, for instance. If possible, it is well worth trying out the platform beforehand or at least checking an online video tutorial on sharing screens, showing film clips, and so on. Other options for using technology in presentations include for instance setting up online polls to gather the audience's vote, or to use apps to create word clouds supplied by the audience or inviting attendees to engage in discussion in the chat window for an online presentation. Again, these can help to create an interactive experience, but a backup plan is always a good idea—and it is worth thinking about how much time explaining the process will take up from delivering the rest of the presentation.

Alongside the use of technology in presentations—but also increasingly interwoven with the art of presenting—is the use of social media during, before, and after presentations. It is becoming rarer that a presentation will be given with no social media engagement at all, though this varies on the context of the presentation and the location. Publicising a presentation ahead of time (e.g., on Twitter) is a common and benign form of social media use; this involves simply pointing to when the presentation will take place and why attendees should join, using the event's hashtag. Livetweeting and other concurrent forms of social media use are also growing in popularity, where attendees of a presentation share key messages, images of the presenter and/or their slides, and juicy quotes from a presentation. This is an interesting area of ethics as live tweeters often do not ask permission to livetweet, but rather assume that, unless a presenter directly requests that no livetweeting happens, it is fine to proceed. When preparing to present, it is therefore a good idea to assume that audience members might tweet their way through your presentation and consider the content of the slides accordingly—or to ask livetweeters not to tweet (or to not take images of the slides). Livetweeting has the benefit of sharing the work with people who are unable to attend the session and also those who are unable to attend the conference. As such it is part of democratising knowledge production and helps to build a researcher's reputation. At the same time, there are risks that are posed to presenters who are working on sensitive and controversial topics—particularly as it is a known phenomenon that women face more online harassment than men, for instance. Balancing publicity with vulnerability is a necessary consideration across academic social media practice, and conferences are no exception. Finally, social media can be used in a more deliberate way during presentations, for example asking audience members to post tweets using a particular hashtag, which are displayed on a side-screen.

4.6 Managing the Q&A session

The Q&A session is perhaps the most feared aspect of giving a presentation. This is the part of the presentation where time is reserved for questions from the audience. The form that this time takes varies and can include an allotted period directly after a presentation, or a shared period grouping together discussion of a set of presentations. Sometimes there are 'questions for clarification' directly after the presentation, followed by a shared discussion after a set of presentations. Questions for clarification are supposed to be short questions to clarify information delivered during the presentation, for instance, an order of events or a type of methodology used. However, sometimes this opportunity is hi-jacked by audience members wanting to get in with their long question or comment—how this is handled is up to the chair. There are advantages and disadvantages to having a dedicated Q&A slot for a presenter and a shared slot across presenters in a session. In a dedicated slot, the presenter is more likely to receive relevant questions that are fresh in the minds of attendees, and each presenter *should* therefore receive at least one question. However, there is also a risk of this Q&A slot being eroded if the session is running late (which may or may not be the presenter's fault!). The advantage of a shared slot is that there is more of a buffer, in that the presenters often all come to the front of the room (or put their cameras on for a virtual presentation), so the single presenter is less exposed. A second advantage is that there may be a livelier discussion as audience members may ask questions that draw out synergies between the presentations. On the other hand, there is a risk that the only questions are aimed at the final presentation or the most senior presenter, or the most provocative paper. If the chair is not attending to an egalitarian use of the time, it is easy for a presenter to be overlooked and to receive no questions.

Because Q&A is a rather unregulated space (depending on the chair) where anyone's concerns can suddenly dominate, it is difficult to prepare for this section! Perhaps the best way of preparing for the Q&A is to present work as often as possible, in different types of events, and to gain experience of fielding questions. There is a first for everything, and the variety of human behaviour that unfolds during Q&A sessions means that even a seasoned presenter can be wrong-footed by a bizarre or confrontational question. Having open expectations of this practice will lead to a more positive experience of Q&A sessions, where an enlightening question or comment is seen as a bonus rather than an expectation. Understanding that, although as presenters we are at the front of the room or the centre of the screen, the audience members are often more concerned about or interested in themselves (unless they have read Section 3.3 of this book!), is a useful reflection—confrontational or antagonistic behaviour is usually more about them than the presenter. A useful practice is giving a presentation in a 'safer' space initially, for example in a doctoral group or department seminar, and encouraging attendees to ask tricky questions. This helps to develop a 'thicker skin', and helps us remember that even if a presentation goes badly it isn't the end of the world. Hopefully, a responsible chair is in place for the Q&A to manage questions and questioners (see section 3.4 on chairing), but it is always possible for a chair to 'turn'—chairs themselves are fellow academics and may forget their role in moderating the discussion and dominate it themselves! Therefore, it is best not to rely on the chair to save the day—developing a professional shell (and a curious ethnographic eye) to move through this interesting academic practice is the best advice we can give. On a more practical level, paying attention to Q&A sessions in an ongoing way (across conferences and other academic events) can help to see what the most common questions are and how others manage the experience.

4.7 Beyond the presentation

Once the presentation is complete and the Q&A session has been traversed, there are just a few final things to pay attention to. Presentations are never quite over when they are over, as they tend to exceed the time and place of presenting in different ways—some of which we can control, and others of which we cannot.

The first of these is the post-session discussion of the presentation. At in-person conferences, this can take the form of one or more session attendees waiting to ask you something or chatting with you at the end of the session. This type of interaction tends to take place in the presenting room or just outside and can be quite tricky to manage as the rules of the session no longer apply. Where to stand? If there are multiple people waiting, who to talk to first? How long to talk to each person? How long to prolong the moment if there are other sessions or lunch to get to? This is where academic bodies at conferences really start to act up—not knowing where to put themselves, getting shy and tangled, un/intentionally appearing rude ... Just having given a potentially nerve-wracking presentation does not always leave the presenter in the best state to coordinate an awkward embodied interaction. One way of managing this type of discussion is to anticipate it (without being too hurt if it does not arise!) and prepare for the unforeseen, almost as an extension of the Q&A. Another way is to voice what is happening—if the conversation seems to be encroaching on a break, you could suggest moving to the coffee area so that the conversation can happen more comfortably; if there is more than one person waiting, you could let the person who is waiting that you will be with them shortly, and so on. These conversations tend to be quite benign, with a further question or a comment on the paper, perhaps a recommendation of a publication to read. However, as with the Q&A, they can be used for academic power play or other forms of power play ... On one occasion, Emily has also got caught chatting with an attendee at the end of her presentation session, who then waited for all the other attendees to leave—at which point it became clear that the predatory attendee was aiming for a romantic conquest of some kind. Leaving the presentation venue quite promptly can be a good idea, depending on what you are open to! However, the post-session discussion can emerge at any time—during breaks or transitions, in the evenings, over email, or even at subsequent events and interactions. This can be pleasing, where a presentation has genuinely made a mark on the audience for the things it made them think about. On the other hand, academic memory can be quite durable in terms of controversies and embarrassments—arguments breaking out during the Q&A, wardrobe malfunctions, social faux pas, and so on. In online conferences, the space for post-session discussions (particularly in terms of the weirdest kind) is more limited, but there is a fairly high likelihood that some discussion will play out in the chat window and/or on social media, or by email.

A second way of thinking about the post-presentation period is seeing it as an opportunity to go beyond the room in disseminating and utilising the presentation opportunity. This can involve writing about the presentation on social media, perhaps offering to write a blog post for the association blog (if they have one) or another relevant blog, sharing the slides file if possible or appropriate (e.g., on ResearchGate), sharing a recording of the presentation if available or desirable on social media or with colleagues. Some researchers keep personal websites or have institutional web profiles that can be updated—adding presentations or links to slides or recordings can be a way of keeping web page visitors up to date with current activities, and may lead to further invitations. Presentations can be listed on the CV (conference date, hosting organisation/institution, location, whether invited/keynote, presentation title, any co-presenter/s) so it is handy to add them just after returning from the conference, avoiding a scrabble for information next time the CV is needed. Finally, a presentation can be used as the basis for a publication or thesis chapter, so thinking of the presentation as situated in a longer trajectory of thinking and writing means that the presentation—and any feedback—have a life beyond the presentation moment.

Presentations can feel like discrete, one-off moments in academic life, that break the rhythms of everyday academic life. They can seem cut off from the rest of what we do. At the same time, giving a presentation is an intense experience which can leave us with all kinds of emotions and confusions—about our work and about ourselves as academics and as people. It can be hard to know what to do with these emotions and confusions. It is important to recognise that the emotions are there, and there are a few ways of mopping up post-presentation affect. Debriefing to others—friends, supervisors, colleagues—can work well and may transform inner turmoil into an opportunity for reassurance and indeed hilarity. If a mutual practice of presentation debriefing is established, this can lead into a satisfying long-term exchange and basis for development and improvement. Another possible strategy is to keep a presentation journal. This suggestion is based on advice that Emily encountered when reading about guest lecturing—that giving a guest lecture, like a conference presentation, can feel disconnected from other kinds of teaching and work. Keeping a guest lecture journal can then connect those disconnected guest sessions and help to develop guest lecture pedagogy (and provide an outlet for emotions) (Henderson, 2019b). An equivalent practice for presenting could help to craft a presentation practice—particularly for those who are more inexperienced and/or nervous presenters—to think about what worked well in terms of preparation and use of technology, but also how it felt to be a presenter in that room/on that screen, on that day.

***

This chapter has aimed to demystify the practice of giving conference presentations, as well as to expose some of the underpinnings of this practice to hopefully allow space for critical thinking around the unspoken norms of presenting. Giving presentations is a practice that unfolds throughout an academic career, and new experiences are always waiting around the corner to be surprising, uncomfortable, and sometimes upsetting— and also banal, uneventful, exhilarating, eye-opening— sometimes all at once. The most experienced presenter can be wrong-footed by things that are beyond their control, such as a misunderstanding about the conference theme or audience or a technology misfunction. While we can never eliminate the unknown future disruption to our vulnerable presenting selves, understanding the conference presentation process and accounting for a range of more probable risks at least means that we have done ourselves a service in advance.

4.8 Further reading: Presenting at conferences

General guides on presenting:

- Becker, L. M. (2014). *Presenting your research: Conferences, symposiums, poster presentations and beyond.* London: Sage Publications.
- Kearns, H. (2011). *Presenting your research with confidence.* IThinkwell.

Specific aspects of presenting:

- **Abstracts:** Burford, J. & Henderson, E. F. (2020, 4 May). Capturing the abstract: What ARE conference abstracts FOR? [Blog post]. *Conference Inference: Blogging the World of Conferences.* Available: https://conferenceinference.wordpress.com/2020/05/04/capturing-the-abstract-what-are-conference-abstracts-and-what-are-they-for-james-burford-emily-f-henderson/ (last accessed 25 January 2022).

- **Posters:**
  - Faulkes, Z. (2021). *Better posters: Plan, design and present an academic poster.* Pelagic Publishing.

- Rowe, N. (2017). *Academic & scientific poster presentation: A modern comprehensive guide.* Cham: Springer.
- **Workshops:** Stanley, J. (1995). Pain(t) for healing: The academic conference and the classed/embodied self. In V. Walsh & L. Morley (Eds.), *Feminist academics: Creative agents for change* (pp. 169–182). London: Taylor & Francis.
- **Accessible slides**: Rector, K. (2019, 7 March). Accessible presentation guide. [Blog post]. *Access: Special Interest Group on Accessible Computing.* Available: https://www.sigaccess.org/welcome-to-sigaccess/resources/accessible-presentation-guide/ (last accessed 25 January 2022).

References

Burford, J. & Henderson, E. F. (2020, 4 May). Capturing the abstract: what ARE conference abstracts FOR? [Blog post]. *Conference Inference: Blogging the World of Conferences*. Available: https://conferenceinference.wordpress.com/2020/05/04/capturing-the-abstract-what-are-conference-abstracts-and-what-are-they-for-james-burford-emily-f-henderson/ (last accessed 25 January 2022).

Connell, R. (2018, June). Survive and thrive 3: How to give a conference paper. [Blog post]. *Raewyn Connell*. Available: http://www.raewyn-connell.net/2018/06/survive-thrive-3-how-to-give-conference.html (last accessed 25 January 2022).

Faulkes, Z. (2021). *Better posters: Plan, design and present an academic poster*. Exeter: Pelagic Publishing.

Henderson, E. F. (2019b). The (un)invited guest? Feminist pedagogy and guest lecturing. *Teaching in Higher Education, 24*(1), 115–120. doi:10.1080/13562517.2018.1527766

Jones, T. M., Fanson, K. V., Lanfear, R., Symonds, M. R. E., & Higgie, M. (2014). Gender differences in conference presentations: a consequence of self-selection? *PeerJ, 2*, 1–15. https://doi.org/10.7717/peerj.627

Kearns, H. (2011). *Presenting your research with confidence*. IThinkwell.
Rector, K. (2019, 7 March). Accessible Presentation Guide. [Blog post]. *Access: Special Interest Group on Accessible Computing*. Available: https://www.sigaccess.org/welcome-to-sigaccess/resources/accessible-presentation-guide/ (last accessed 25 January 2022).
Rowe, N. (2017). *Academic & scientific poster presentation: A modern comprehensive guide*. Cham: Springer.
Stanley, J. (1995). Pain(t) for healing: the academic conference and the classed/embodied self. In V. Walsh & L. Morley (Eds.), *Feminist academics: Creative agents for change* (pp. 169–182). London: Taylor & Francis.

5 Organising conferences

Figure 5.1 'Registration desk' by Rhiannon Nichols

5.1 Why organise a conference?

There are many reasons why people decide to organise a conference. Often these reasons are not particularly glamorous or intellectual. Many conferences are organised simply because of an inherited expectation of a regular conference, which is the case with academic associations and learned societies. Others are convened because a research project proposal included the promise of a conference—and why did the research

DOI: 10.4324/9781003144885-5

proposal include that promise? Because conferences are a recognised, symbolic form of knowledge dissemination; a conference organised means an objective met, with evidence to provide to the funder. This is perhaps a cynical view of conferences. Still, it is also important to recognise that many conferences are organised without a real sense of *why* they are being organised, and this has many knock-on effects for those involved both in organising and attending. Sometimes a conference is organised by the person who can be leant on to agree to do it—because of status and/or personality (and/or intersecting identity characteristics—who does the academic housework?). Academics organising conferences may not be the people who have the right skills and disposition for event organisation—and many conferences are organised with insufficient administrative support. Some academics decide to organise a conference because this ticks a box on promotion criteria and serves as a means to enhance their academic reputation—they would like to *have organised* a conference but are not that keen on actually organising it. Conferences are also organised for other purposes such as developing a new research agenda, project, or publication; disseminating findings from a completed project or publication; developing networks; sharing knowledge and practice; promoting an institution, association, or network; creating and sustaining a research community that is meaningful to them; or inducting new members into the field. These aims feed more directly into the knowledge production potential of conferences, and can be underlain with more passion than the purposes of habit, fulfilled promise, and personal career enhancement—though it is important to note that there can be multiple purposes playing out both within a conference organising team and within an individual who is involved. As with many things in life, individuals involved may have more or less awareness of their own desires when it comes to volunteering to organise a conference.

An overarching concern with each and every purpose outlined here is that academics do not tend to know how to organise conferences well. A whole events industry of training programmes, courses, and professionals exist—including academics working in this field and researching event organisation. However, a great number of academics and doctoral students set about organising conferences without consulting other sources or working with conference professionals, and many conferences are patched together simply on the basis of other conferences that people involved have attended and organised in the past. Many conferences are organised without reference to texts on organising conferences. Conference organisers who do refer to texts are likely to come across the 'how to' genre, where top tips are given to organise a 'good' conference. Many blog posts, short articles and some books are produced in this vein, often by academics who have organised conferences themselves—who often also have no idea that there is literature out there to draw on. The cliché 'reinventing the wheel' comes to mind! Given the assiduous attention to working with existing research and scholarship in the academic profession, it is perhaps surprising that relatively few conference organisers engage their 'research brain' for their conference. Indeed, many academics we have met along the way have been flabbergasted by the idea of researching conferences, as it had never occurred to them that, while intricate aspects of a farming technique only employed in a remote community somewhere or other have been exhaustively researched, conferences too could be both researched and organised in a research-engaged way.

Academics who have access to plenty of resources may consider simply outsourcing the organisation of a conference to an events professional. This may result in a well-organised, slick conference, but the conference professional cannot engage in the field-specific aspects of the conference, so can only work to a universal template of 'what works'.

What we are suggesting in this chapter is that academics who are considering organising conferences, but who feel ill-equipped, dispassionate and/or stale, can direct some of their intellectual passion for their academic work into organising a conference. Organising a conference can be an enlightening, inspiring experience, which teaches organisers more about their research interests and also about the nature of their field. Equally, it can be an exhausting, fractious, even divisive experience which can lead to chaos and stress that detracts from any potential benefits to the organisers. By being honest about the ways that many academic conference convenors enter into conference organising, we are trying to (re)inspire a more engaged mode of conference organisation. While conferences may often be planned and organised along practical, functional lines, this chapter conceives of organising conferences as *curating spaces*, by which we mean thoughtfully designing spaces with intention as to the experience that they create for attendees. The curation of these spaces then impacts on how attendees experience the conference, whether they will return (if it is a recurring conference) and indeed how they are socialised into academia. The objective of this chapter is to supplement existing 'how to' advice with a more critical discussion of conference organising. The chapter moves through each stage of conference organising: establishing the conference aims and a conference design that aligns with the aims; considering the roles and approaches to organising a conference; developing a conference pedagogy; choosing conference components; planning for the practicalities of conference organisation; evaluating the conference.

5.2 Aligning conference design with conference purpose and aims

It may seem bizarre to state this, but many conferences are organised without a clear purpose or defined aims. This results from the fact that, as discussed above, conferences are often organised out of habit, or to fulfil a promise to a research funder. Perhaps the purpose of a conference appears to be obvious, but a lack of preliminary discussions on purpose and aims can lead to a disalignment between purpose, aims, and conference design. Disalignment happens more often than we might hope, and this can produce a disorientating, unfocused conference experience for attendees. We can think of a few different occasions where we have put in substantial effort and resources to attend a conference, only to find that the conference was somehow *not right*. The spirit of a conference is an intangible, ephemeral notion, but anyone who has attended a conference with a toxic or confused spirit will immediately know what we are referring to. Embarking on organising a conference can often leap straight into the logistics, but is well worth pausing at the very start and discussing the purpose and aims. For a regular association conference where the organising team rotates to a different organising team and host for each conference, eliding this step is particularly common. This can lead to the reproduction of stale and indeed exclusionary conference practices. As an organiser of one of these conferences, it can feel impossible to challenge the norms because the ownership of the conference is shared with the association. However, it is still possible to discuss the purpose of this particular instance of the conference, and to come up with aims that perhaps aspire to shift some of the norms or to make a particular statement. It is also a good idea to reengage with the question of why a regular conference is needed at all. For conferences that fulfil promises made to research funders, again the purpose can seem obvious, but in fact these conferences are often founded on loose aims such as 'to disseminate the project findings'. One-off, specialist conferences are more likely to have a clearly defined aim, but equally this aim may reside in one person's mind and not be shared among the organising team.

By conference *purpose*, we mean *why is this conference being organised*. Each set of purposes leads to a different set of aims and a different set of decisions for the design of a conference. It is worth being honest about the purpose of the conference. If the conference is simply occurring out of habit or to fulfil a promise, it is worth acknowledging this and then taking design decisions accordingly. Pretending otherwise can lead to an unnecessarily complex event which can become burdensome and cause friction in the team. In our view, it is better to acknowledge the original purpose of the conference and then consider how the conference can be beneficial within that scope.

Conference *aims* are more specific than the overall purpose, and also challenge conference organisers to think ahead to their priorities for an event, and how these can be realised. Aims are potentially measurable in some sense, and the organiser should be able to evaluate the meeting of the aims in the post-conference period. The aims should be related to the purpose but can also go beyond the purpose.

The conference *design* should then match the aims and purpose. It is easy to get distracted by what we think a conference *should* look like or what success means. For instance, aiming for quantity of attendees can easily eclipse—and contravene—a conference aim of furthering specialist discussion. Thinking through indicators of success is important, even if they are indicators that are hard to measure, such as creating an inspiring or inclusive space. Likewise, inviting a fancy keynote can also eclipse the conference aim if the keynote does not respect the theme of the conference—sometimes inviting a less fancy speaker but thinking about success in terms of engagement with the theme might mean that the conference is more productive. If an aim is to create an international conference, holding the conference in a country with racist border controls (as opposed to choosing another country or holding the conference online) may directly contradict the aim. As you can see, this is a complex space. We will now work through some more specific examples to demonstrate how purpose, aims and design can become (dis)aligned.

5.2.1 The regular conference

The purpose of a regular conference may be to showcase cutting-edge research in the field, to bring together a community of scholars, to redefine the priorities of the field, and to socialise new scholars into the community.

As an example, Emily was, at the time of writing, the academic convenor of the annual doctoral conference that is organised by a committee of doctoral researchers in her department. This is certainly a conference that is organised out of habit, arranged with the (previously unspoken) *purpose* of socialising doctoral students to conferencing and providing a safer space for students to practice presenting. The conference *aims* were therefore to organise a recognisable conference that would give students a flavour of conferencing, and to provide opportunities for as many students to present as possible. Further aims were added of aspiring to attract a range of presenters and attendees from other departments and other universities, and of organising a conference with a clear set of inclusive conferencing principles. The conference *design* was influenced by the aims, in that it took the form of a traditional conference, and was designed to accommodate a large number of speakers presenting in parallel sessions (instead of being selective).

5.2.2 The pre-promised conference

The purpose of a pre-promised conference may be to satisfy funder requirements, to ensure that other scholars and/or practitioners are aware of the project findings. As an example, at the time of writing, Emily was also involved in organising a pre-promised conference for a research project she was involved in. The *purpose* of the conference (again unspoken) was to demonstrate the academic credentials of the project to the funder and partners, to gain legitimacy for the project in the country context where the project was set, and to disseminate project findings. However, the organising team did not explicitly agree on the purpose and aims at the start of the process, in part because the date and format of the conference were affected by the COVID-19 pandemic, and it became something of a race to get the conference wrapped up during the project duration. Thinking back through the purpose and the aims, the *aims* became rather diffuse and potentially contradictory, with additional aims creeping in such as attracting as many presenters as possible, shoring up an international partnership relationship that was somewhat unclear, introducing the research team to other colleagues working in the area, engaging in capacity-building for the junior members of the team and early career presenters, ensuring a diversity of research being presented across the field… These differing aims were guarded by different members of the team located in different countries, and they repeatedly surfaced during phases of conference organisation (where it was too late to rectify them). This was a clear example of where a pre-promised conference elided the discussion of purpose and aims, resulting in a rather bumpy and stressful organisation process for all members of the team. The *design* of the conference was influenced by the pandemic, so required to move to an online format, which confused the original purpose of consolidating an international partner relationship. The design was also influenced by perceptions of success which, due to the diffuse aims, were more related to what a conference *should* involve (which turn out to vary across country contexts and disciplines—not easy for a transnational cross-disciplinary conference), rather than to the project's specific purpose and aims. However, despite the issues identified here, the conference somehow seemed to meet many of these contrasting aims and was a highly successful event.

5.2.3 The ad hoc conference

The purpose of an ad hoc conference may be to bring together scholars working in a disparate or marginalised field, to develop a specialist area of knowledge, or to bring together collaborators in order to work on a joint publication or research project bid. As an example, a couple of years prior to the time of writing, Emily mentored a team of doctoral students to apply for funding for and then organise a specialist research symposium with a methodological focus. The purpose was clearly defined as bringing together researchers who were working with a marginalised method to enhance the community and the organising team's own network, and to promote the method to others who had not come across it. The aims were clearly aligned with the purpose, as the team had no particular need to organise this event and it was driven by our passion for the method. The team also discussed the event in detail, in part prompted by the funding application pro forma. For this event, the team located and invited authors whose work we had engaged with as well as new contacts working with the method. The team also aimed to attract others to the event who had not come across the method. A further aim was for the doctoral students involved in the organisation to learn how to organise a conference. The *design* of the conference was influenced by the aims, in that it was set up as a small, one-day event which would therefore be manageable for interested researchers to travel there and also would not be too onerous for attendees who would sign up out of curiosity. The design of the event also sought to balance inducting attendees to the method and developing the knowledge of more experienced attendees, so we included a range of presentations and incorporated group tables and workshop elements in order to facilitate interaction between attendees.

The main point we are trying to make here is that a preliminary discussion about purpose, aims, and design can set the basis for a meaningful conference, where all concerned are proceeding with a united sense of what the conference is all about. It also means that the discussion can be returned to as a reference point if things are going awry with the conference organisation process. Finally, it means that ideas that everyone holds about what counts as a successful or a proper conference can be surfaced and discussed, hopefully ensuring that compromises are made, or that consensus is reached early on in the process rather than appearing later in the form of disagreements. Organising a conference is never completely smooth, but initial discussions which also engage with the intellectual endeavour of hosting a conference are certainly an advisable way of getting more out of what is inevitably a challenging process.

5.3 Roles and approaches of conference organisation

Organising a conference can be one of the most exciting professional activities that academics engage in. The process can form friendships and collaboration relationships among the organisers. Rather like flatmates who are thrown together to coexist and jointly manage a property, conference organisers have to work together through an intense, unpredictable and potentially volatile process (Burford, Bosanquet & Smith, 2020). And just like flatmates: they can end up becoming friends for life or find each other intolerable by the end of the organising process. This is not surprising—conference organisation places extra labour on the people involved, and the reward of this is often rather opaque and generally un- or under-remunerated. Moreover, it is a demanding process that can eat up time and destabilise work-life balance. Different people manage their time and their work-life balance differently, with some people having more flexibility than others, and some people bearing more of the emotional responsibility for a conference. Working together in an intensive way reveals people's priorities and where their boundaries are—this can be a joyous realisation of a shared or complementary working style or a sad or angry realisation of differentiated commitment or incompatible ways of working. Co-organising a conference, then, involves a significant amount of labour on the part of organisers. It is wise to be honest about this in the first instance, and to ensure that all conference members involved are available at peak times—or if their availability will be limited, that they are not playing a key role that depends on a particular kind of availability. Of course, things happen, and it is not always possible to predict emergencies, but at least commencing with an honest conversation about availability provides a starting point for balancing the labour.

As with many aspects of conferencing that we are discussing in this book, we are advocating a more thoughtful approach to conference organising. Many conferences are organised in an automatic way and miss out on preliminary conversations about the purpose and aims—and how these connect with the conference organising team. We hope that, by being more intentional about forming the team, there will be more lifelong friendships formed and fewer bust-ups. A key question to ask at the start of the process is: who will be involved in organising the conference, and why?

Often conferences start with one person or a couple of people who are in convening a conference, and who are then joined by others to form a team or committee. The leadership of a conference is then shared between the members of the team, with different forms of decision-making and different leadership structures being enacted, depending on the conference. However, there is usually someone who has the last word, or who is the last link in the chain of responsibility—and, in practice, this may or may not end up being the same person as the conference chair. We have both contributed to conferences where the responsibility has been somewhat diffuse or confusing, and as such we set out some principles here which we think could lead to a more reassuring conference organisation process.

A conference chair, in our view, has an overarching role of keeping the show on the road—overseeing that the conference is at the stage it needs to be and that meetings are occurring as and when they should be, and setting the agenda (with the potential for others to contribute to this, of course). A conference chair can also keep sight of the intellectual aims of the conference, in terms of its contribution to the field, especially when other team members may be bogged down with logistical challenges. This also applies to keeping the conference organisation process in view, ensuring that ethical commitments are met. Sometimes, a conference chair may need to make a final call or suggest a vote when a process has stalled. We see a conference chair as taking responsibility, as holding the conference with care, empathy and kindness, not as someone who is out there on their own issuing orders. Successful conferences we have been part of have involved a chair who recognised others' strengths and encouraged others to lead on certain aspects, who trusted the committee members and empowered them to act, who expressed gratitude and thanked others for their time and labour (physical and emotional). Perhaps it may seem antithetical to leading a conference, but we think that a conference chair needs to be aware of their own limitations, and to know when to ask for help, as an overwhelmed or defensive or over-tasked chair has less availability to step in to help with a team member's struggles. We also think that a conference chair needs to listen as well as speak and needs to set a culture of respect.

A conference chair should be someone who has availability in terms of time and also emotional capacity. Additionally, it is helpful if it is someone who has relevant experience of leadership, and ideally, of conference organisation. It is possible to create a leadership structure where the intellectual development of the conference is conceived by an academic (conference chair or convenor), and the practical leadership is overseen by another person (conference manager) who could be an events professional or—as is often the case, for better or worse—a postdoc or junior member of staff. Sorting out early on how the leadership structure will work is a good idea, as letting this fall into place during the process can lead to misunderstandings and resentment as de facto leaders feel obliged to step in to save a floundering process. When the committee or team is formed, it is important to discuss the experience levels and leadership strengths of those who are expected to be involved, to check that no one is given responsibilities that are far beyond their current level of experience or availability. While organising a conference is a great way of developing as a junior researcher, if the more experienced members of the team do not have time or space to curate that

Organising conferences 121

development process, it may be better to shape the roles around current rather than aspirational capacities.

It is impossible to include all the different leadership formations that can occur around conferences in this chapter, as conferences are so diverse in this regard (from massive association conferences to tiny departmental symposia). However, a basic principle is that the leadership—of the whole process and of different aspects, including committee responsibilities—needs to be established at the outset and the roles need to be discussed with frankness and deliberate thought about what is involved.

The leadership of a conference is interwoven with but also distinct from the list of practical tasks involved. Again, this is a discussion which needs to be prioritised at the start of the process, as the conflation of leadership with practical organisation (in the sense of micro-managing or taking over tasks from others who are perfectly capable) can lead to a bumpy ride! Just because a conference chair is bearing the leadership of a conference does not mean they have to do the bulk of the work—though it also does not mean they are exempt from the labour either. A conference chair needs to be in a position where they can keep sight of the overarching aims of the conference and ensure that the tasks are happening as they should, so that they are also available to help where a member of the team is struggling or take on a task in an emergency. A conference chair who is already too heaped up with tasks cannot play this role, so establishing a feasible workload for the chair and committee members is an important early step in the process. Of course, different conference teams work in different ways with vastly different numbers and levels of resourcing. Some conferences are organised with full-time paid staff working on the job, and others are organised by one or two individuals and perhaps a handful of student volunteers. While setting out all the different configurations is not possible in this chapter, a general principle is to conceptually disentangle the leadership from the list of practical tasks, so that overall responsibility for the conference can be guaranteed as well as the successful completion of the tasks involved.

It is becoming a refrain in this chapter that conferences are often organised by people who find themselves in that position for various reasons, rather than die-hard conference fans. This has the effect that many conference chairs are just aiming to 'get it over with' and to ensure that the conference is not a total disaster. While this may be the case, this chapter endeavours to inspire academics who find themselves in that position to set about the task in a more intentional way, with the view that this can lead to a more satisfying (and less traumatic) process. An important point here is that a chair's leadership style for organising a particular conference may not be the same as other areas where they lead. There can be deliberate differences. For instance, an academic who usually likes to work with a hands-off style, allowing members of a research group to explore and take their own time, may decide to adapt to a more hands-on style for a conference that needs to be organised with a short timeline and has accompanying success measures that need to be met for a funder. This can be conveyed to the team by explicitly stating that they may notice some difference to the usual way of working, which is due to the specific circumstances of this conference. Unlike in many professions, where leadership training and continuous professional development are compulsory and highly structured, academia takes a looser approach and many academics are reluctant leaders. Engaging in some reflexivity about how we usually (try to) lead and thinking about whether those principles are applicable to the conference that needs to be organised is a basic starting point. Consulting with leadership manuals and models is a more in-depth task but could be worthwhile in the long run, in order to experiment with different ways of doing things. Another possibility is asking other conference chairs about their experiences—and thinking about how conferences you have attended have worked—in order to help to build up a cumulative picture of conference leadership.

A final point here is that the approach taken to organising a conference can reflect different principles on the part of the organiser/s. While much conference organisation is dominated by a strategic approach—trying to get things done with success measures in mind—there are other ways of doing things that reflect additional priorities. There is increasing attention to this aspect of conference organising, where considerations of inclusivity are rightly inching up the agenda. This is discussed in greater depth in Chapter 6. However, it is important to note that conferences that *only* take a strategic approach are contributing to reproducing—and even exacerbating—negative aspects of the status quo in academia. Adopting a more ethical approach does not have to lead to huge amounts of extra labour and can make a positive contribution to the field. A conference can be led from this perspective, and it is perhaps surprising that academics do not always (and often do not) apply the principles that they adhere to in their research and teaching to their conference organisation. For instance, organising a conference on care but holding conference committee team meetings at school pick-up time … It is more common than one might think to lead a conference overlooking this type of consideration.

Leading a conference and serving on a conference committee can be a landmark moment, forging friendships and indeed influencing others' practices around conference organising. It is therefore worth putting some detailed thought into who will lead and why, and how they will lead, and who will be involved in the practical organisation, what they will do, how and why. Perhaps it sounds rather simplistic, but we argue that conferences that are organised with intention are more likely to be successful and rewarding—and hopefully to contribute to transformation rather than reproduction in the academy.

5.4 Conference pedagogy and mode

As discussed earlier in this chapter, it is remarkable that many academics organise conferences without engaging their 'research brain'. Many academics have considered their teaching philosophies and preferred pedagogical approaches, which are underpinned by years of experimentation and academic reading. Conferences can be seen as a form of teaching—in terms of curating a learning experience for attendees. In fields that have established teaching pedagogies, there has been some attention to applying those principles across to conferences. Feminist pedagogy is an example, where principles of feminist pedagogy are often considered at Women's and Gender Studies conferences. Of course, there are many different interpretations of feminist pedagogy, but some core principles that translate across to conference organisation involve challenging academic hierarchies, arranging the conference space to allow for more interaction and participation, and including diverse voices from within and beyond academia (Belliappa, 2020; Saul, 1992). Other pedagogical decisions relate to critical pedagogies which seek to destabilise norms; this can translate into decisions about conference organising such as using an unconferencing format, which decentralises the conference presentation/pre-defined topics as the basis of interaction instead often involving higher levels of spontaneity and attendee interaction and participation (Dunford, 2018). Jamie has been involved in unconferences in the past, often in the context of activist or international development gatherings, where there has been a clear commitment to generating self-organising groups to consider complex and interconnected social issues. As we see it, thinking about conference pedagogy is an important way of moving from a technical and strategic process to an intellectual, critically engaged endeavour.

Closely linked with conference pedagogy is the question of mode, referring to in-person, online and hybrid modes of conferencing, which is a pedagogical choice. The decision is often taken on the practical grounds of *can the people who need to be there get there?* Nothing has shown that more clearly than the COVID-19 pandemic. However, choice of mode—and how that mode is implemented—shape the conference experience at a deep level, and each mode has its compromises in terms of the purpose and aims of the conference at hand. Questions of access collide with questions of physical co-presence; these thorny issues are discussed at greater length in Chapter 6. In choosing the mode, it is necessary to consider the intended delegates in parallel with the aspirations of the conference, as more effort may be required to achieve those aspirations. In an online conference, for instance, more creative thinking is necessary to curate incidental networking spaces, if that is an intended part of the conference. In a hybrid conference, working out how to avoid a segregated conference takes more work. In an in-person conference, working out how to create inclusive networking spaces that are not dominated by alcohol poses its own challenges. In an online or hybrid conference, decisions about synchronous versus asynchronous content are also decisions about inclusivity and pedagogy, but these imperatives may pull in different directions. As we go on to argue in Chapter 6, there is no perfect conference, but taking decisions about mode as pedagogical (as well as practical) decisions ensures that the decisions are taken in the most thoughtful manner possible.

5.5 Conference components

Conferences may be more or less complex in nature and can involve a range of different components. With the growth of the conference industry and the academic profession, there is more competition between conference providers to bid for conference contracts, and between different academic associations and conference organisers to attract attendees. Although the COVID-19 pandemic interrupted the industry and conferencing practices, the race for market share transferred into online conferences, and in the post-pandemic era there will surely be new developments and directions for competition. The basic point though is that attendees tend to have high expectations in terms of both in-person and online conferences, because they are allocating valuable financial and/or time resources to the events. The larger association conferences have become overwhelming affairs with a plethora of different activities on offer, driven by a growth mentality and/or the drive to engage in more ethical and inclusive practices. In designing the conference, this is where some of the distractions can occur that deviate from the conference purpose and aims, due to other measures of success or previous experiences that creep in. '*If we don't do that, people might ask questions*'; '*Oh that was good, we should do that too*'. There are many decisions to take about conference design, and as noted earlier, there are many 'how to' guides that can accompany the process (see recommendations for further reading at the end of this chapter). Rather than replicating these guides, this section provides an overview of some of the choices that need to be made and why some options might be selected, with a view to helping conference organisers to stay faithful to the purpose and aims of the conference. Deciding which components to include and how they should work is a question of balance—what is the balance of different components sought for the conference at hand—but also the topics of the previous sections in this chapter should be retained and threaded through these decisions. Deciding on an over-complex schedule where there is insufficient motivation and staffing to successfully deliver on that schedule, for instance, is best avoided. Simplicity may provide a more meaningful experience, if that simplicity feels pedagogically crafted.

As discussed in Chapter 3, conference presentations tend to be the basic foundation of conferences, with the schedule designed around fitting in the requisite number of presentations. There are decisions to be taken about the extent to which presentations *should* form the dominant activity at conferences. On the one hand, moaning about boring and incompetent conference presentations—and too many of them—is a staple of academic banter. On the other hand, often conference funding is contingent on presenting; limiting the presenters to just a few and/or to invite-only may limit the audience and also reduce the potential for democratic knowledge production. Secondly, while unconferencing and other experimental and interactive conference techniques are becoming more popular, we have also heard academics moaning about attending conferences where they just wanted to relax and listen to some work, as a break from having to 'perform' as teachers all the time, and academics who have objected to having to contribute the curriculum of the conference through, for example, flipped classroom techniques. Including presentations is likely to be a necessity, but there are different options, and these should be aligned with the conference purpose and aims. There can be options for longer and shorter presentations; for attendees to be grouped and/or to group themselves by proposing symposia; for the presentation of formal papers that are submitted before the conference, which may entail a full presentation or a short presentation with the assumption of the paper having been read before the conference; for the presentation of work in progress and/or discussion in, for example, round tables that attendees can propose; for workshops and experimental sessions (see, e.g., Benozzo et al., 2019).

In relation to any of these formats, there are decisions to take about which voices can and should be heard at the conference, what the attendee experience is imagined as, not to mention the administrative burden of any of these options and/or these options in combination. Is the conference team in a position to be flexible if they are contacted with suggestions for alternative formats—if they say yes to an additional/experimental format, can they deliver on offering the conditions for that suggestion to be realised? Conference organisers also have to make tough choices about selectivity. An invite-only conference is the epitome of a selective conference—however, this may be necessary for a specialist conference with a limited budget and a stated purpose of collating ideas for a book project. With any open call, there are decisions to take about the reviewing of abstracts and papers. Reviewing is a labour-intensive practice that needs to be planned for, and reviewers benefit from having clear criteria that are interlinked with the conference purpose and aims. Conference abstract reviewing—like any peer reviewing—is a gatekeeping practice that polices the boundaries of a field. It is also labour intensive and difficult to monitor for fairness. However, without any reviewing process, there are risks regarding the relevance of presentations—and a smaller conference may need to be selective in order to be able to deliver on a successful, well-coordinated event.

Another cornerstone of conferences are keynote speakers (Peseta, 2018). Traditional conferences include keynotes in the programme, where renowned academics and well-known figures deliver longer presentations and are usually scheduled as plenary events, where all attendees are encouraged or expected to attend. Generally, keynote speakers are not presenting on a particular project, but rather are discussing the conference theme, which is likely to be related to their area of expertise. They are generally invited on an expenses-paid basis and may be offered an honorarium. Keynote invitations are often included in promotion criteria, and are recognised as a measure of academic career success. However, there are also increasingly arguments against featuring keynotes in the traditional sense. While some keynote presentations are referred to as defining moments of a discipline, and a good keynote sticks in the mind forever, they are also another source of academic grumbling, due to the fact that the floor is given to a single speaker for an extended duration, often with a somewhat diffuse topic. Some conferences take the decision of not including any keynote or plenary items. It depends on the type of contribution to the field that the conference is trying to make, as a keynote can, as a productive conference component, have the effect of summarising the state of play, furthering the field or contesting ingrained aspects of the field. Ways of spicing up the plenary sessions include inviting provocative speakers, arranging a panel of short presentations instead of a single speaker, inviting less predictable speakers. Matching the plenary with the purpose and aims of the conference is essential—and it is important to consider that a keynote rarely 'makes' a conference, but they may well 'unmake' a conference if their talk and/or style is dull, stale or even prejudiced or discriminatory.

In addition to the presentations and keynote/plenary sessions, there are many other components that can be considered. Increasingly, conferences are engaging with artists and poets, with graphic recording of conferences (where a cartoon-style depiction of the papers is produced in real-time and often shown on a live screen—see Osborne, 2019) and poets in residence (producing poetry that is inspired during the conference) are hired to enhance the creative aspects of conferencing. There are also other kinds of sessions to consider, such as 'meet the journal/book series editors', workshops on topics such as publication or public engagement, book launches, and 'in-conversation with' sessions. Conferences also often include entertainment and cultural programmes, including film screenings, performances, outings and visits (including virtual visits), and art exhibitions. The social and networking aspects are a key part of scheduling, including break times with refreshments, formal dinners and drinks receptions, networking sessions (e.g., research 'speed dating'). Finally, running alongside the main schedule there is often a marketplace or exhibition where relevant organisations and publishing houses have stalls to recruit members or sell their wares. All of these elements can be offered in online conferences, although the online versions tend to be attempted replications of in-person activities, which meet with more or less success. This list of components is bound to be incomplete, but even in this brief section, the list is long and overwhelming. Moreover, these are political decisions that have implications. Different stakeholders may have different ideas about what should be included—for instance a women's studies conference that Emily attended in India included both a woman-centred rock band and a highly gendered display of 'local' cultural dances, which stemmed from different interests and different priorities—and resulted in a rather contradictory message being conveyed to the bemused delegates! It is important to return to the purpose and aims of the conference, and to the notion of *thoughtfully curating* a conference. A conference does not have to include all these elements to be successful, and indeed a chaotic, crammed schedule may produce a stressful conference experience for all concerned. Designing a conference within the means and capacity of the organising team, with a reasoned selection of elements (and potentially narration of this selection to the attendees) is probably a better guarantee of success.

5.6 Practicalities of organisation

As with conference components, there are myriad choices to make when it comes to the practicalities of conference organising. Again, 'how to' guides set out different ideas and logistical solutions for conference organisers (see recommended resources at the end of the chapter), and these can be consulted for in-depth advice on how to go about organising a conference. However, we suggest that these guides may be approached through the lens of thoughtful conference curation, and with the conference purpose and aims front and centre. There is no recipe for a perfect conference and no universal system that will work. Practicalities are the focus of this section, but for each logistical topic, we include consideration of how conference practicalities are also political and ethical decisions about inclusion. These issues are discussed in greater detail in Chapter 6, particularly regarding inclusivity and the geopolitical nature of conference organising in international academia.

A first important consideration here is that, while there are some universal things that make a conference recognisably a conference, no matter where it is held, conferences vary hugely across different contexts. Conferences are inevitably infused with local customs and politics, and given the differences in academia across different regions, it is unsurprising that conferences too are open to contextual interpretation. Conferences held in the Global North—particularly the US, the epicentre of the academic conference industry—may be taken as setting norms and standards, and many conference organising guides are written from the US and the UK. Indeed, academics travelling from metropole locations to conferences in so-called peripheral destinations may impose expectations that emanate from that US-based 'standard' and complain if their expectations are not met. We have both witnessed privileged academics whom we admire hugely for their ethical approach to research become alarmingly demanding at conferences hosted in Global South locations. We too are writing this book from a Global North location, but we would urge conference organisers, no matter where they are, to consider how a conference can reflect something of the location where it is embedded, rather than aspiring to identikit conferences. Some of the ways in which conference practicalities may differ pertains to welcome ceremonies (e.g., welcomes by Indigenous communities, felicitation with garlands or gifts), to the place of hierarchy and formality (e.g., whether it would be insulting not to invite a senior leader of the host institution to attend, whether titles should be used or not). It also extends to other questions such as how the food is served and presented, whether alcohol is served or not, how the accommodation is set out, the style of conference social and entertainment programme, and provisions for and timetabling around religious observance.

Organising conferences has different phases, and it is essential to consider each phase along with the purpose and aims of the conference. In the conference organising timeline, funding is an important consideration to be taken way in advance of the conference. Considering what funding would be needed for and where it could come from shapes the nature of the conference. It is possible to host a conference without any funding, but this limits the scope for the event—an unfunded conference could, for instance, take the form of a half-day event in a classroom on campus, with the expectation that all speakers and attendees are either local or able to self-fund their travel, and with notices about bringing own refreshments. It is easier to organise an unfunded online conference, but this requires plentiful availability of the conference team (with their time funded, e.g., through their usual salary). Conference funding can range from a small sum covering basic refreshments and local speaker travel to huge budgets that include venue hire, staff hire, transport, food, accommodation, international speaker expenses, and payment—and sometimes gifts for speakers, bursaries for students, the unwaged, retired attendees, and so on. Conference funding may be sought via an internal funding scheme, embedded into a larger research grant, and/or sought via sponsorship. The basic point about conference funding is that funding itself creates labour, usually requiring a detailed application, careful budget management and accountability, and reporting after the event. This relates back to the conference team (Section 5.3), as a team with insufficient capacity and/or expertise will struggle with an unwieldy budget. Having a huge budget can be overwhelming and mean that the original aim of the conference is lost amid trying to design a spectacle. Decisions about which funding to apply for, and how much, should therefore be taken with a clear view of what the conference is for, and who will manage the funding process.

Another set of practical decisions unfolds around the location of the conference, including venue and/or online platform, accommodation, food, and registration. Each decision is accompanied by implications for the conference experience, and it is worth stating at this point that each one of these decisions is politicised. In terms of online conferences, there are questions of 'location' in terms of the time zone/s that the conference will operate in, as well as localised preferences for different online platforms which may work more or less well in other country contexts. It is worth establishing who and where the potential audience for the conference is, and organising the conference schedule around at least the dominant time zones (and potentially including these time zones in the schedule), and providing clear guidance on how to use the chosen online platform. In terms of in-person conferences, the politics of location is an important issue. Where a conference is held says something about the conference itself. Choosing a location for a national conference is a power-laden decision, and there is an established practice of 'conference ambassadors' (Rogers, 2019) who assist with bidding for conferences to be hosted by particular cities and/or venues, because of the important source of income that large association conferences bring to local areas. In the arts, humanities, and social sciences, conferences may be located with reference to the topic or discipline; for instance an Indian conference that Emily attended was located in the North-East region of India in order to stake a claim for the inclusion of this often sidelined region in the national discipline. The NWSA (National Women's Studies Association) conferences in the US tend to be in 'second-tier' cities because the accommodation and services tend to be less expensive in these cities, which is a feminist principle of inclusion. Choice of venue is equally a political issue, as shown for instance by choosing a university campus, versus a corporate hotel, versus a venue established as a community collective. A campus may seem appropriate for an academic conference, but campuses are sometimes difficult to get to by public transport. Lining the pockets of a corporate hotel may seem unethical to some delegates, but these hotels are often built with higher levels of accessibility. A community collective venue may seem more ethical, but may be difficult to reach by public transport and may be less well equipped for deaf delegates, for example. As a reminder, there is no perfect conference, and each decision has implications for inclusivity for a different group. However, at least articulating the justifications for the decisions taken—including narrating these to the delegates in the conference materials—leads to more thoughtful conference organising.

The provision of food and accommodation at in-person conferences is a thorny issue (see also section 3.7 from the delegate perspective) and one that is also intimately connected with conference registration fees. Conference hospitality differs widely between conferences, and each conference will be experienced differently by different attendees who come with different expectations, requirements, and norms. The most thoughtfully curated conference will likely come across to at least one delegate as negligent in some way. This is not an excuse to leave these things unconsidered, but again to emphasise that the decisions that are taken should be taken thoughtfully and ideally narrated to attendees in the conference materials. In a conversation with two catering managers at Emily's university conference centre, she explored the thought process that goes on behind food planning for conferences. They said that, for instance, the recent requests for vegetarian- or vegan-only conference fare was meeting with issues from some attendees who felt unsatisfied by the sudden diet switch. That the request for healthy-only food (e.g., fresh fruit instead of dessert) was disappointing to some who had come to the conference expecting to have a 'treat'. Some conferences do not provide any food, instead signposting nearby providers, or only provide small snacks. These decisions depend on budget and the ability to serve food and drink in the selected venue. Not providing food may bring the registration fee down, but may also feel unhospitable and create issues for session attendance if attendees are constantly required to leave the venue to seek food (and then get distracted from the conference in doing so!). Likewise with accommodation, choosing a venue with available accommodation increases the likelihood of full conference attendance, but at the same time often the accommodation associated with a conference venue is above a reasonable price for many attendees. Sometimes accommodation is included in the fee; sometimes there is an add-on option; sometimes local hotels from different price ranges are included in the conference information. With both food and accommodation, it is essential to consider the nature and needs of the specific intended audience for the conference, but also to retain flexibility for additional requests. Seeking the views of a small number of potential delegates at the planning stage can be a good idea, if time allows, as this may reveal hidden assumptions within the organising team (e.g., assumptions of car ownership, of dietary preferences, of alcohol-based socialising).

Based on these decisions, whether, how much, and how to charge for conference attendance is a key question. Charging for conference registration includes a combination of covering costs and anticipating attendee thresholds (see Section 2.4 from the delegate perspective). Some conferences charge a notional fee in order to improve the chances that registered attendees will attend, as free conferences have a notoriously low conversion rate of registration to attendance. This makes organisation (particularly of in-person events) very difficult as there is a reliance on the laws of probability, meaning that there is always a risk of having too many or too few attendees. However, charging a fee is also complex, labour-intensive, and requires systems in place (again we come back to the organising team, see Section 5.3), and may be somewhat inappropriate, for example, for an unwaged audience. If the funding allows, hosting a free conference may be the easiest route. Conference fees vary enormously, and they may be used to cover the staffing time for organisation, for instance, which may appear invisible to attendees. We advocate for the clear justification of conference fee rates to delegates, for example, presenting a pie-chart in the conference publicity showing what the fee will be spent on (and ideally showing that it is not for profit!). Including different fee rates for different groups is another political decision, and again varies by context, but often includes students, unwaged, retired, independent researchers, and/or attendees from low-income countries. In some cases, there is fee remission and even a number of bursaries for travel, accommodation, and care support. Again, it is important not to follow a universal script here—considering the purpose of the conference is vital, as there may be groups that the conference would like to welcome that require a specific fee structure.

Finally, all conference organisers need to pay some attention to risk management and contingency planning. This is discussed further in Chapter 6, particularly with reference to the fragility of conferences that has been revealed by the COVID-19 pandemic, but conferences have always been open to some risks. At the basic level, organisers can plan to have staff who are trained in first aid rostered at the conference, as well as a list of numbers for emergency services available (or included in conference materials). It is also good practice to have a clear understanding of the evacuation procedures if there is an emergency (e.g., earthquake or fire) and a plan for any duties that conference staff might need to play in making sure all delegates exit safely. All conferences are at risk of presenters not showing up, through illness, through transport or visa issues, through internet issues or power outages (for online conferences). The highest risk is the keynote or plenary speakers not being able to attend, and a contingency plan is vital here, particularly if the speaker is travelling a long way or is a 'big name' and known to be unreliable. We have both attended conferences where the keynote has been replaced at the last minute—by another speaker or even by an impromptu picnic. This can be tricky if part of the appeal of the conference was to hear that particular speaker, and their absence can lead to a sense of let-down and disappointment pervading the conference, so it is important to plan for this eventuality and to take into consideration how the conference is marketed (with more than one selling point!). It can also be tricky to invite another person at the last minute who might feel they are the substitute for the star, so it is advisable to proceed with tact, perhaps even inviting a trusted colleague to step into the keynote's shoes. Other eventualities may occur—the conference being cancelled, or attendees being unable to travel to the conference, or attendees being unable to leave the conference. These eventualities may occur due to political unrest, changes in visa rules, or even volcanic ash clouds that put a halt to international flight departures (Jensen, 2011)—as well as epidemics and pandemics playing havoc with our abilities to plan ahead and execute our plans as desired. Some of these eventualities can be planned for—and some contingency is always necessary, for example establishing funding conditions with the funder if monies have been irretrievably spent for a cancelled conference and considering how to move a conference online at the last minute. However, some eventualities cannot be planned for, and conference organisers always need to ready themselves for this fact.

5.7 After the conference: Evaluation and beyond

Hosting a conference—actually living through it and getting to the end of it—is a massive achievement, no matter what the conference is. Doing so always involves curating a complex web of processes with different actors who have different priorities, and this is also accompanied by people's emotions, fears and anxieties as well as—hopefully—joy and pleasure. As a first point for the post-conference period, then, we would recommend scheduling a celebration with the organising team. Once a conference is over, it can often feel like a relief, and, because a conference is ephemeral in nature, it can just feel 'done with' as it fizzles out on the day. Ensuring that the team has a get-together in the diary to celebrate and debrief and pat each other on the back is an important part of conferencing and something that can be done with an online team as well as in person.

Conference evaluation is another post-conference consideration. Again, it is important to think about whether an evaluation is needed, why, and how it will be implemented, as evaluation is labour-intensive. If the conference is a recurring event, then figuring out how to improve it next time is worthwhile, or if there is a need to report on the success of the conference to the funder, then this may necessitate an evaluation, but with different types of questions. Conference evaluation can be app-based, sent as a web questionnaire, and/or a paper form handed out at the event. An at-event evaluation may be wise in terms of capturing attendees' views before they leave and forget about the conference, but at the same time attendees may be more able to think about their experiences having gained some distance from the event. The evaluation needs to be planned in advance, including who will process the data and how it will be reported on—often conference staffing is set up with the conference itself as an end date, so extending into the post-conference period is a good idea to ensure that there is staffing for this process.

There are other ways in which conferences are extended beyond their day and time. Some resources—and energy reserves—need to be set aside for these tasks, and it is wise to get these planned and scheduled during the momentum of the pre-conference period, bearing in mind inclusivity issues of who does the labour and/or who gets the glory for this work. Thank you notes need to be sent to speakers, volunteers, and other key actors. Payments and expenses need to be sorted out. Websites need to be closed or edited to be a static archive. Conference proceedings or reports need to be produced and edited if part of the plan. Next steps are discussed, for example, an edited book or project if that was the intention of the conference—and sometimes as a natural progression of interesting discussions at the conference. Conferences continue to be discussed on social media platforms for a short time after the conference, and then, in the longer term, there may be blog posts or conference reviews published in journals (e.g., Grant, Burford, Bosanquet & Loads, 2014). Conference organisers can engage in some of this activity themselves, actively stewarding the online discussion and reporting on the conference experience in blogs or reflective articles. This depends on the energy and inspiration of the conference team members, and as to whether this has been planned in advance so that the momentum is retained. As discussed earlier in the chapter, some conferences end on a positive note, and others end with lasting rancour... This also affects who decides to do what in the post-conference period, and it is not the end of the world if a conference does not produce outputs of this kind.

Part of the post-conference moment is also thinking about how the conference went, as it sinks into line with all other conferences attended and hosted. Reflecting on the experience then shapes how future conferences will be attended and hosted, and so the informal knowledge base that predominates in the world of academic conferences is accrued. In this chapter, we have advocated an approach to conference organising that involves *thoughtfully curating* conferences—engaging our 'research brain', thinking through each decision and justifying it rather than following a universalising script, and narrating the 'why' of various decisions to attendees—respecting them as knowledgeable beings. In turn, we hope that this approach leads to a more solid knowledge base for academic conference organising, with less 'reinventing the wheel' and more of a sense of contributing to a community of practice.

5.8 Further resources: Organising conferences

- Bos, A. L., Sweet-Cushman, J., & Schneider, M. C. (2019). Family-friendly academic conferences: A missing link to fix the "leaky pipeline"? *Politics, Groups,*

and Identities, 7(3), 748–758. doi:10.1080/21565503.2017.1403936
- Burford, J., Henderson, E. F., & Pausé, C. (2018). Enlarging conference learning: At the crossroads of fat studies and conference pedagogies. *Fat Studies, 7*(1), 69–80. doi:10.1080/21604851.2017.1360666
- Chautard, A. & Hann, Claire. (2019). *Developing inclusive conferences*. Oxford: School of Geography and the Environment, University of Oxford. https://www.geog.ox.ac.uk/about/equality-diversity/190522_Inclusive_Conference_Guide.pdf
- Clark, D., & McDonald, G. (2014). *Organising an academic conference: Guidelines for scholarly and financial success*. Prahran: Tilde University Press.
- Hansen, T., & Ren, C., (2020). Chairs of academic events: The investments and academic impact, *Science and Public Policy, 47*(3), 322–332. doi: 10.1093/scipol/scaa007
- Kelly, K., Yiu, L., & Vanner, C. (2020). Toward a feminist framework for virtual conferencing. *Comparative Education Review, 64*(4), 769–776. doi:10.1086/710770
- Reshef, O., Aharonovich, I., Armani, A. M., Gigan, S., Grange, R., Kats, M. A., & Sapienza, R. (2020). How to organize an online conference. *Nature Reviews Materials, 5*(4), 253–256. doi:10.1038/s41578-020-0194-0
- Segar, A. (2015). *The power of participation: Creating conferences that deliver learning, connection, engagement and action*. Marlboro, VT: Conferences that Work.
- Terzi, M. C., Sakas, D. P., & Seimenis, I. (2013). The contribution of the scientific committee in the development of conferences. *Procedia – Social and Behavioral Sciences, 73*(Supplement C), 373–382. doi:https://doi.org/10.1016/j.sbspro.2013.02.064

References

Belliappa, J. L. (2020). Extending feminist pedagogy in conferences: Inspiration from theatre of the oppressed. *Gender and Education, 32*(1), 101–114. doi:10.1080/09540253.2019.1646412

Benozzo, A., Carey, N., Cozza, M., Elmenhorst, C., Fairchild, N., Koro-Ljungberg, M., & Taylor, C. A. (2019). Disturbing the AcademicConferenceMachine: Post-qualitative re-turnings. *Gender, Work & Organization, 26*(2), 87–106. doi:10.1111/gwao.12260

Burford, J., Bosanquet, A., & Smith, J. (2020). 'Homeliness meant having the fucking vacuum cleaner out': The gendered labour of maintaining conference communities. *Gender and Education, 32*(1), 86–100. doi: 10.1080/09540253.2019.1680809

Dunford, M. (2018, 12 March). 'UnTold'—lessons from an unconference. [Blog post]. *Conference Inference: Blogging the World of Conferences.* Available: https://conferenceinference.wordpress.com/2018/03/12/untold-lessons-from-an-unconference/ (last accessed 25 January 2022).

Grant, B., Burford, J., Bosanquet, A. & Loads, D. (2014). Of zombies, monsters and song: The third Academic Identities Conference. *Teaching in Higher Education, 19*(3), 315–321. Doi: 10.1080/13562517.2013.860113

Jensen, O. B. (2011). Emotional eruptions, volcanic activity and global mobilities—A field account from a European in the US during the eruption of Eyjafjallajökull. *Mobilities, 6*(1), 67–75. doi:10.1080/17450101.2011.532653

Osborne, R. (2019, 24 March). Graphic recording—engaging audiences at conferences. [Blog post]. *Conference Inference: Blogging the World of Conferences.* Available: https://conferenceinference.wordpress.com/2019/03/24/guest-post-by-rebecca-osborne-graphic-recording-engaging-audiences-at-conferences/ (last accessed 25 January 2022).

Peseta, T. (2018, 4 June). Keynotes: Starting conferences with a bang or a whimper? [Blog post] *Conference Inference: Blogging the World of Conferences.* Available: https://conferenceinference.wordpress.com/2018/06/04/guest-post-by-tai-peseta-keynotes-starting-conferences-with-a-bang-or-a-whimper/ (last accessed 25 January 2022).

Rogers, T. (2019, 25 February). Conference Ambassador Programmes. [Blog post]. *Conference Inference: Blogging the World of Conferences.* Available: https://conferenceinference.wordpress.com/

2019/02/25/guest-post-blog-by-tony-rogers-conference-ambassador-programmes/ (last accessed 25 January 2022).

Saul, J. R. (1992). Planning A Women's Studies Conference. *Feminist Teacher, 7*(1), 22–25.

Segar, A. (2015). *The power of participation: Creating conferences that deliver learning, connection, engagement and action*. Marlboro, VT: Conferences That Work.

6 Thinking about conferences

Figure 6.1 'Thinking about conferences' by Rhiannon Nichols

6.1 Thoughtful conferencing

So far, the chapters of this book have focused on different aspects of conferencing, and we have threaded through critical insights and points of discussion and debate, to inspire readers to think about conferences in different and hopefully more critical ways, and even to change what they do. This chapter is designed to extend the thinking

DOI: 10.4324/9781003144885-6

and arguments presented in the previous chapters, with the idea that readers who reached for the book for a specific purpose (e.g., organising a conference) might be tempted to engage in more in-depth consideration of conferences. The chapter, therefore, presents an invitation to think critically and ethically about conferences and to be more thoughtful in conferencing practices. By 'thoughtful conferencing' we mean asking questions about the received norms of conferences, thinking about how conferences benefit some people more than others, considering how conferences reinforce, reproduce, and even exacerbate inequalities in the broader higher education sector, placing conferences in the broader landscape of the world and evaluating their impact on wider social and environmental issues… Through the chapter discussions, we introduce and model different ways of thinking about conferences. Though there is no such thing as a perfect conference, we encourage greater reflexivity in conferencing practices and more acknowledgement—to ourselves and others—of why particular decisions have been taken. The chapter encompasses four sections, each taking a different angle on conferences: conference inclusivity and belonging; democratisation of knowledge production and circulation; environmental and sustainability concerns; the fragility and resilience of conferences.

6.2 Conference inclusivity and belonging

Throughout the chapters of this book, we have alluded to the ways in which conferences are unequal in and of themselves, and how they connect with inequalities in the academic profession at large. Many different terms can be deployed to signal these discussions. 'Inclusivity' and 'belonging' are the terms we have chosen, though we are aware that different terms are used in other contexts and that there are many critiques of this type of 'equality and diversity' terminology as being apolitical, euphemistic, even depoliticising (Ahmed, 2012). Our use of the terms inclusivity and belonging is strategic—to argue for the consideration of conferences as spaces that need intervention, as the inclusivity agenda in academia is often applied to institutional structures only, thus omitting conferences. However, conferencing success is closely tied to career success due to the tangible benefits (e.g., presenting or organising are forms of evidence used in promotion cases) and the many intangible benefits (e.g., enhanced reputation, consolidation of collaborations, development of ideas). As such, we argue that neglecting questions of access to and within conferences from the broader inclusion debate is a serious omission. The term belonging is used in educational debates to signify that inclusivity is not limited to facilitating the inclusion of excluded groups into existing spaces and structures but rather shifting the norms so that excluded groups feel a sense of belonging. What we mean by an inclusivity and belonging agenda for conferences is to consider the different ways in which people are included and excluded from conferences—not only from attending them but also from participating fully in them while attending, and to think about how conference inclusivity can be more actively practiced. Consideration of the conference 'curriculum' is also vital within these debates; as signalled by the decolonising the curriculum movements (Manathunga, 2018), inclusion relates to knowledge and forms of knowledge production as well as bodies in the room. For us, the inclusivity and belonging agenda for conferences is not limited to conference organisers but is relevant to all the aspects of conferencing that are covered in this book, with the responsibility for inclusive conferencing lying with all of us.

We are suggesting, then, that conference inclusivity and belonging enter into:

- preparing for conference participation (see Chapter 2),
- participating in conferences (see Chapter 3),
- presenting at conferences (see Chapter 4),
- organising conferences (see Chapter 5).

Alongside these different aspects of conferencing, there are several different axes of in/equality to consider, including among others:

- gender,
- caring responsibilities,
- sexual orientation,
- race/ethnicity/marginalised and minoritised groups (e.g., caste, indigenous groups),
- social class,
- religion/faith,
- dis/ability,
- language,
- nationality,
- age,
- academic seniority/contract status.

Meanwhile, for each of these, there are considerations of both:

- inclusivity (facilitating access),
- belonging (feeling welcome/at home).

Adding all these possible intersections together then, it is clear then that there are at least 88 starting points for discussions about conference inclusivity and belonging … This is an overwhelming prospect and it is perhaps not surprising that lethargy sets in around these issues, especially since conferencing is already challenging without paying attention to this plethora of concerns. However, we cannot afford to ignore these concerns, as we are all implicated and most of us are affected by conference in/equality at some point. Our aim in this section is to provide a way into thinking about conference inclusivity and belonging. As such, we mention a select number of concerns related to the axes of in/equality listed above, with the caveat that the list of axes and the lists of concerns are far from comprehensive. We have provided further resources for digging into these issues further at the end of the chapter.

One of the most common discussions about conferences and inequality surrounds who is invited to speak at conferences, for how long and what about. Terms such as 'manel' (a panel with only men speakers) and 'whanel' (a panel with only white speakers) have been coined to refer to the ways in which conferences reinforce the prestige of privileged groups at the expense of recognising the diversity of the academic profession. Protests against manels and whanels have become more common, and some academics publicise turning down invitations to speak on exclusionary panels. Boycotting has become a strategy in this regard, but it is important to remember that the capacity to refuse an invitation may more available to the already privileged. Another strategy of protest is to attend the conference but boycott the session or to stage a walkout. 'No-platforming' is another area affecting speaker choice. For example, people who have a record of being transphobic or from a group with extremist views may be blocked from speaking at conferences by a variety of actors including the academic association, the hosting institution, and the delegate mass. This area attracts fierce debate as no-platforming is often pitted against freedom of speech and academic freedom, with different groups with different allegiances fighting for different corners depending on their priorities. Speaker choice is most often debated in terms of the keynote/plenary speakers, as a conference organiser's issue. However, it is also important to remember that there are decisions that individual presenters make in terms of inclusion and/or recognition of co-presenters, co-authors, research assistants, as well as decisions for anyone who is organising a round table or symposium within a conference. In short, anyone participating in knowledge production at a conference can contribute to the conference by thinking about these concerns when making key decisions during the process.

While speaker choice sets the tone for a conference and demonstrates the commitments of a conference to, for example, representing scholarship from marginalised groups, establishing a sense of belonging involves paying attention to detail within the conference. Many of these responsibilities fall, in principle, to the conference organisers, but in practice much responsibility falls to other attendees and contingent staff such as volunteers and servers. A conference committee can set inclusive practices up, but they cannot always control the implementation of those practices. For instance, it is perfectly possible to set up a conference policy on the inclusivity of trans and non-binary delegates, but for gender policing to occur in bathrooms and misgendering to occur in the coffee queue. A committee can establish and distribute a no-tolerance to racism or sexual harassment policy. Still, nonetheless a conference delegate may mistakenly assume a person of colour is a server, or a delegate may experience predatory behaviour during a drunken conference dinner. This does not, of course, mean that conference organisers should skip attending to these issues, but that conference attendees should also be cognisant of the limits of organisers' control, due to the unpredictable and sometimes anarchic nature of conferences as temporary, transient spaces.

There are different degrees to which a conference can facilitate access and/or promote belonging. Organisers can set the tone of the conference by putting in place codes of conduct around discrimination and harassment, and can make these more or less prominent to attendees by announcing them in the conference welcome or displaying them clearly on the website and programme. There can be visible sources of help and support at the conference, including sexual harassment officers wearing marked clothing or lanyards. Organisers can also set the tone of the conference by signalling inclusivity through food provision (e.g., providing kosher and halal fare), providing childcare services (e.g., conference creche or information on local childcare providers), allocating spaces for prayer and/or spiritual practices, allocating a breastfeeding room with a fridge, providing gender-neutral bathrooms, ensuring there are at least some social activities that do not revolve around alcohol, ensuring that a quiet room, ramps/lifts, and sign-language services are in place. While any of these provisions can facilitate a sense of belonging, some can also inadvertently impede a sense of belonging. For instance, having to request kosher or halal food from busy servers, not being able to use the creche as it is only for very young children, having to walk halfway across the site to find the prayer room, breastfeeding room, gender-neutral bathroom, or quiet room and missing sessions to do so, finding that the alcohol-free event is empty as it is held at the same time as a popular drinks reception, having to travel out of the main thoroughfares of the conference in order to find the lifts/ramps ... any of these attempts to facilitate belonging may also backfire. Moreover, differences between contextual norms mean that different priorities surface. Conferences in countries with different dominant religions have different norms about when a conference is possible or undesirable, and these unspoken calendars may collide with international guests' calendars. There may be different levels of stigma and even legal provisions attached to different groups, such as LGBTQ+, members of Indigenous communities, or unmarried women, which affect the extent to which attendees are made to feel welcome. Again, none of these complexities constitute excuses to give up on trying to create an inclusive event, but rather we view this list as a reminder that people are complex, and bringing them together in a transient space is particularly challenging, as there is little chance to adapt or remedy once the conference is underway. One of the best things a conference organising team can do to promote inclusivity is to be both approachable and flexible, though these attributes require ample resourcing.

As attendees and presenters, there is a shared responsibility to contribute to ethical conferencing by being good conference citizens. There are many simple ways of being at a conference that may be helpful to others. For instance, approaching people who are wandering around alone looking lost, speaking clearly while presenting and while conversing with people who may be hard of hearing or who speak your language as an additional language, reading and writing out quotes on presentation slides, providing a written version of the conference presentation to the audience, checking with people you are including in an informal dinner that the restaurant works for them—and being mindful of different income levels (sometimes splitting the bill is not fair!), querying assumptions before assuming a fellow attendee's gender (e.g., avoid using gendered language such as 'ma'am' and resist asking people if they are in the right bathroom), sexual orientation (e.g., avoid assuming that someone's partner is of a different gender to them), nationality, age, seniority and so on. As noted above, a conference may have an explicit inclusivity agenda and may do its best to create a sense of belonging, but there is only so much control that can be exerted, and a sense of acceptance or belonging can be shattered in an instant by someone who is not even connected with the conference. It is worth thinking about culpability in these issues, and this is a thorny issue for conferences. Where does the conference begin and end? At the airport, the train station, the car park, the hotel that has been recommended, the venue, the presenting room, the café in the venue, the streets surrounding the venue, on social media—which parts are the responsibility of the conference organisers? In online conferences, how the chat window is regulated has also become a contested space, due to the potential for polemic discussions to erupt during a presentation. Does the chat window belong to the organiser, presenter, or audience? Sometimes chat windows are not even made available due to the risks. There are ways in which conferences can create structural conditions for inclusivity and belonging, but the micro-level interactions with other attendees and personnel and even passers-by constitute the fabric of the conference, and this is where regulation stops and wildness sets in.

Conference inclusivity and belonging is a huge area for further thought, and we have only scratched the surface here. We end this discussion with a consideration of one further aspect, which we refer to as 'diversity decisions'. By this, we mean decisions that are taken—on the macro-level of the conference organisers as well as individual attendee decisions about how to be at the conference—to facilitate inclusivity and belonging for one axis of inequality, but which then have ramifications for other inequalities. For instance, where bursaries can be made available, there are decisions to take as to who can apply for a bursary. A care bursary might be selected at the expense of a bursary for students or for attendees from low-income countries. There may be one spare room that is available, resulting in a decision between using it for a prayer room or children's playroom. There may be enough budget for a sign-language interpreter *or* an interpreter for an additional language. Holding a conference that works with different time zones may mean that attendees who have to do the school drop-off or pick-up are excluded from key sessions. From our extensive research on conference inclusivity, we have found that every inclusivity-motivated decision that benefits one attendee results in the disadvantaging of another attendee, via the opportunity costs associated with these decisions. A diversity decisions approach asks conference organisers and attendees to explicitly think about the implications of decisions they make and to aim for an ethical form of conference citizenship, while at the same time recognising that there is no possibility of perfection in this regard.

6.3 Democratisation of knowledge production and circulation

Closely linked with questions of conference inclusivity and belonging are issues of the democratisation of knowledge production and circulation. Here we are referring to questions of how conferences interact with marginalised knowledges and marginalised knowledge producers, whether in a particular context or on a global scale. This section taps into debates about decolonising the curriculum and interrogating postcolonial dichotomies of metropole and periphery (Connell, 2017), as well as neo-colonial forces that are shaping the international higher education sector such as university rankings and increasing monopolies of publication houses (Dawson, 2020). Conferences sit in an uneasy position in relation to these debates. Undeniably conferences in the Global North, particularly the vast association conferences of the US, are held up as the global standard of conference. This is then reflected in the unequal weighting of these conferences on academic CVs and in promotion applications in other parts of the world. And yet it is common knowledge that citizens of many countries struggle to obtain a visa to gain entry to many countries in the Global North (Nshemereirwe, 2018), and the costs of travel, accommodation and subsistence are beyond most academics' financial capacities (both in terms of self-funding and gaining institutional funding). Moreover, abstracts are predominantly reviewed within the metropole, meaning that different styles of knowledge production or projects focused on so-called peripheral country contexts are more likely to face rejection for conferences that are becoming fiercely competitive in nature. Researchers have studied the so-called 'international' conference circuit and have found that it is far from international in nature (Derudder & Liu, 2016; Dubrow et al., 2015). At a national scale, the hierarchy of institutions and regions produces a similar situation, with more rural and remote areas forming the periphery to an urban elite metropole in the capital city and other hotspots of knowledge production. A project explored the distribution of conferences in Jordan, for instance, and found that almost all conferences were located in the same few locations (Alananzeh et al., 2017). Many academic commentators on social media have asserted that online conferences open up conference attendance, which is in many cases true, and yet it should still be remembered that access to the appropriate technology and internet facilities is unequally distributed and many of the same (often unintentional) gatekeeping practices that keep Southern knowledges out of conferences may endure.

A key focus of the democratisation agenda is the exposure of the exclusion of academics working at the 'periphery', and an attempt to ameliorate this through direct measures such as financial assistance and invited speakers, both at national and international scales. The conference curriculum also enters the scene here, in terms of which topics and forms of knowledge production are acceptable or welcome at conferences. The call for papers is perhaps the most important source of inclusion or exclusion in this regard. The themes and topics as well as the options for different types of presentation are all listed in the call for papers, demonstrating to potential attendees what is expected or welcomed, and the extent to which there may be flexibility in terms of topic and/ or form. If the call for papers also includes the topics or at least the profiles of the keynote speakers, this also sets a tone. What does the call for papers tell us about the conference? Will radical or controversial topics be accepted at this conference?

The democratisation agenda also includes who is welcome at conferences in terms of different stakeholders. Conferences have traditionally been the domain of fully-fledged academics, with some inclusion of postgraduate (especially doctoral) students, though students are often scheduled for unpopular slots and/or shorter presentations. Other students (undergraduate and Masters) may hardly get a look-in, though there are sometimes deliberate attempts to invite student groups along, as well as some conferences specifically for undergraduate or high school students. Some conferences give a clear message by inviting a student union officer to contribute to a plenary panel, demonstrating that the conference in question values student voices as well as more traditional academic expertise. Likewise, some conferences also make clear attempts to include voices from beyond the academy, such as politicians, activists, and NGO representatives, and so on. In medical or other hybrid academic-professional conferences, this mixing of speaker provenance is the norm. Some fields struggle with ethical questions as to whether and how to include participant groups from research studies in conferences. Fields with an explicit social justice agenda—where participant voice and agency are prioritised—still often exclude key actors from conferences. For instance, Rosie Barron (2020) writes about a conference on sex work where sex workers were excluded from attending and staged a protest at the conference boundary. At a recent online conference that Emily attended, one of the speakers invited members of the marginalised group she had researched to attend her presentation, which they did, despite not being able to understand the language spoken at the conference—the presenter said they were intrigued to just be part of the experience, but the gesture also opens up many questions about the un/translatability of academic research across different potential audiences.

While conferences are often held up as undemocratic spaces, it is also necessary to recognise the crucial role that conferences also play in democratising knowledge production. Taking the field of feminist research, conferences have been documented as vital sites where feminist knowledge has been formed and legitimised, despite institutional and mainstream disciplinary opposition. This applies both within national contexts (e.g., Krishna's 2007 account of an Indian Association for Women's Studies workshop) and where international conferences have brought together feminists from different countries to compare notes on their equivalent struggles (e.g., Basch's 2001 account of gatherings in France and the US). Conferences provide opportunities for minorities to temporarily form a majority. As such, while managing to gain access to that temporary space may be highly challenging, conferences play an important role for minoritised and marginalised groups—in terms of identity and also in terms of research field—and they provide important arenas for the showcasing and development of fields that may otherwise be trampled down and even stamped out.

6.4 Environmental and sustainability concerns

The global conference industry has in recent years come under increasing scrutiny in terms of environmental and sustainability concerns. Conference travel is highly inefficient, as it often entails travelling very long distances for a short duration. In larger countries such as Australia, India, and the US, or nations comprising many islands such as Indonesia or Malaysia, even attending domestic conferences often involves air travel. The carbon footprint of conference travel is eye-wateringly large (see, e.g., van Ewijk & Hoekman, 2021). It is difficult to conduct a cost-benefit analysis of conference travel, as conferences have many indirect and intangible benefits which cannot easily be pitched against a carbon calculator. Arguably, long-distance conference travel should be avoided at all costs in an attempt to reduce academia's contribution to global warming. A clear solution to this is online conferences, which have a much lower carbon footprint. Before the COVID-19 pandemic, there was a great deal of resistance to online conferences, but through necessity, the academic conference industry adapted to hosting and participating in online conferences with rapidity and willingness. Through the pandemic period, academics have found ways of networking online and bridging (some of) the geographical divides that worldwide travel restrictions opened up. However, it remains to be seen whether this embracing of online conferences is here to stay, or if it will wane in favour of a return to in-person conferences. Many social media commentators have said how much they miss in-person conferences, due to the multiple distractions and competing priorities that accompany attending online conferences at home or in the office, and due to the sociable experiences and embodied connections that can only occur at in-person conferences. This is known as 'meetingness' (Elliott & Urry, 2010), and this ephemeral, mysterious conference vibe is missing from—or only very faintly present at—online conferences.

Thinking about conferences 161

There are therefore questions as to how the pleasure and intensity of in-person conferences can be replicated online—or whether environmental concerns should force the profession to find other ways of hanging out and thinking together.

Aside from the online conference as a solution to conferences' carbon footprint, there are other ways of altering conferencing with environmental and sustainability concerns in mind. One option is to change the mode of transport. More academics in the UK context, for instance, are being urged or even required by their employers to travel by train or other public transport to conferences. Of course, this is balanced against other issues such as how many days different academics can manage to be away—academics who do most of the care work in their departments and at home may be disadvantaged by these policies. Some conferences and/or departments organise car-share arrangements or minibuses, but this relies on the conference being relatively nearby and the academics living near enough to the university to all take the same bus or car. There is increasing discussion that academics should be seeking out more local conferences, rather than annual pilgrimages to US association conferences, for instance. It is certainly the case that, in our experiences, attending a small-scale, specialist conference that is relatively nearby can be extremely rewarding. Multi-site conferences are being trialled, where academics travel to one of a number of sites which are also connected to each other through some virtual elements (King, 2019). This is an exciting prospect. However, there are some obvious pitfalls to both local and multi-site conferences. Many academics worldwide are located in sprawling countries with highly dispersed universities, meaning that most academics—except for those in the metropole—do not have 'local' conferences within reach. Academics who live on islands may not be able to travel without air travel due to the distance by sea from other destinations. Second, changing the coordinates of the conferences map cannot happen independently from the coordinates of institutions and indeed the global higher education sector. While conferences still serve as indicators of international reputation enhancement in promotion criteria and international collaboration in university rankings, avoiding attending them is not an easy option—yet, how to bring about change? Top down? Bottom up? Thirdly, if local conferences are the solution, surely this will lead to the (re)formation of knowledge silos … Yet we cannot engage in ethical conferencing without taking into careful consideration the impact of conference travel on the environment.

A second major concern—specifically for in-person conferences—is in relation to sustainability issues at conferences. The scale and short duration of conferences have led to unsustainable practices such as the use of single-use plastic and food waste. Moreover, the power needed to heat or cool huge venues, often with lights left on constantly, is a great environmental concern. The ways in which these issues are addressed varies hugely across national and regional contexts, especially because conference venues are more or less tied into national sustainability policies (e.g., recycling). Increasingly venues are also marketing themselves on a sustainability basis, and in the conference industry, 'green conferences' are becoming a phenomenon, where particular attention is paid to, for example, energy, waste, water, biodiversity and ethical products. In the events industry, sustainability is a recognised challenge. Events tend to be transient, temporary phenomena, but require facilities that make people feel comfortable and catered for. Where people are staying away from home, they require bedding and towels and food and vessels for eating food, especially if they have travelled by air with cabin-only baggage allowance ... and then, a few days later, they do not require these items anymore. Sustainable practices can collide with financial priorities, as greener practices are often more expensive. For instance, using reusable dishes for conference catering requires more staff labour and the capacity to store, transport, and clean large quantities of crockery, than disposing of paper and plastic items. Since many conference providers are trying to keep costs down in order to provide a service that is affordable to as many attendees as possible, taking decisions that increase costs has knock-on effects for inclusivity. However, there does seem to be a drive to reduce the material impact of conferences at many conferences we have attended, such as by only printing programmes on request, providing a reusable water bottle and water dispensers, encouraging attendees to use one set of towels for their stay rather than requesting a new set each day, selling off remaining food at a reduced rate to students on campus at the end of the conference day or organising a food bank collection, and so on. It is also the responsibility of attendees to take these matters into their consideration, as there does sometimes seem to be a tendency for conference delegates to drop their usual principles of sustainability while they are away—though admittedly it can be rather frustrating traipsing around a large venue in order to find somewhere to refill a water bottle! Thinking about conference waste, then, will only become more of a pressing concern, but for now there are two main suggestions we have: ask questions from the organisers (e.g., in association open meetings held at conferences), and practice usual sustainable habits to the extent possible even when away at conferences.

6.5 The fragility and resilience of conferences

The nature of conferences means that they are relatively high-risk endeavours. They are temporary and transient and therefore rely on a set of people coming together—online or in person—at the specified time and in a specified way. There are many ways in which parts of conferences are susceptible to being disrupted, and indeed whole conferences are also sometimes affected. Organising a conference is a huge undertaking, and yet there is a distinct possibility that at least something will go wrong: bracing for this is part of the process of organising and attending conferences. Common eventualities relate to the services that surround conferences, such as issues with catering turning up at the right place and time, online platforms not having been set up for slide sharing by presenters, or presenters not being able to attend and thus creating gaps in the schedule. Keynote speakers are a particular liability, particularly those who are travelling long distances to arrive, as they may be affected by travel disruption or visa issues—or, if they are 'rockstar' academics, may consider the conference as just another day and cancel at late notice if they are feeling unwell or over-stretched. In online conferences, keynotes may be susceptible to getting the wrong time or not managing to connect to the correct platform. Keynote speakers can also be disruptive by running over time, presenting on something irrelevant and/or provocative (not necessarily

Thinking about conferences 165

in a good way!), or giving an insultingly short talk that they have clearly prepared in the cab between the airport and the conference venue. There are also risks related to other elements of conferences, such as the planned entertainment not showing up, or the technology failing for a film showing, or wifi not working in the venue, or something going wrong with the toilets ... Not to mention deliberate disruptions such as boycotts, protests, walk-outs, sit-ins, social media campaigns, Zoom bombing, and so on. The result of diversity decisions (see section 6.2)—around logistics as well as conference curriculum—can end up with at least some attendees having a terrible conference experience, with attendees feeling offended, excluded, marginalised, or even being hospitalised due to a lapse of control related to an extreme foodstuff allergy. Conferences are risky endeavours, and their success depends on a fragile mix of structural planning, attendees who get along, and luck.

In addition to parts of conferences being open to various disruptions and failures, whole conferences are also susceptible to being cancelled. While the COVID-19 pandemic brought about the most public, mass cancellation of conferences, there have been many other reasons for conference cancellation over the decades—as well as for attendees to get stuck in the location where the conference was taking place. For instance extreme weather events such as hurricanes lead to conference cancellation (Campos, Leon & McQuillin, 2018); political instability such as terrorist attacks (Boger, Varghese & Rittapirom, 2005) and political manoeuvres (Carpay, 2001) lead to sudden changes of border control for incoming and outgoing travellers. Because conferences are organised over a fairly long-term calendar, sometimes set in advance by as much as four years, they are vulnerable to sudden shifts in conditions. COVID-19 was not the first health crisis to disrupt conferences—the SARS epidemic for instance led to some conferences being cancelled (Kang, Suh & Jo, 2005). However, the COVID-19 pandemic, due to its global spread, certainly revealed the fragility of the conference ecosystem. Conferences were cancelled from the start of 2020 with alarming alacrity, leaving organisations, providers, and academics alike in a state of confusion and panic. The event industry is a major employer, with many staff who work on zero-hours contracts according to the ebbs and flows of people through the events calendar. Many academic commentators have found much to celebrate about this move to online conferences, including their sustainability benefits, as well as their creative use of digital tools for conference presentations, the possibility to listen to recordings of conference talks before and after the actual conference, and possibilities to reduce power hierarchies in virtual environments where young scholars may find it easier to raise questions or approach senior colleagues online than in person. Online conferences may seem to be more resilient, but sudden internet outages and power outages due to any of the above-mentioned conditions can scupper the best-made plans. Moreover, many event industry workers lost their livelihood as a result of the shift online. As conferences expert Judith Mair (2014) points out, academic conferences are important sources of income for convention centres and their surrounding communities because conferences take place all year, meaning that employment is maintained even out of the traditional tourist high season. The fragility of in-person conferences to health (and other) crises is interlinked with the precarity of the events industry workforce, a fact that has been overlooked in the academic social media commentary about the impact of COVID-19 on conferencing.

Conferences, then, are a fragile phenomenon. However, they are also a resilient phenomenon—academics seem to find ways of continuing to conference even when the conditions seem impossible. Individual academics move heaven and earth to attend conferences, even when all the odds are stacked against them, and even when the benefit of attending can never match the personal and financial investment. The pandemic has also demonstrated the resilience of conferences, showing that academic conferences do not take long to shift mode or form according to the possibilities. Online conferences were already taking place a month or so into the COVID-19 pandemic, and they mushroomed through 2020 into 2021, with the associated seismic adjustments to conferencing practices taking place over just a few months. Accompanying the sudden switch to online practices has been a huge growth in writing about online conferences, with many academics publishing blog posts and short-form journal articles about their experiences of and guidance on online conferences (for a selection of these, see the end of this chapter). It remains to be seen how conferences—and their organisers and attendees—will shift in the wake of the pandemic, and whether inclusivity and sustainability concerns will remain on the agenda as conference travel seems more possible again. What does change with health crises and indeed political instability is the perception of risk, and how increased risk shapes conference organising and attending patterns. There is of course never a universal degree of confidence that conferencing plans will come to fruition, as some academics will never face the same level of certainty as others—depending on nationality, for instance, or dis/ability. The remarkable thing about the COVID-19 pandemic was that it disrupted the conference travel of all academics, including the most privileged, globally elite academics who are used to flitting around the world with a cloak of invincibility, introducing an element of doubt and risk even to their hitherto unstoppable trajectory. How this ubiquitous risk will be managed in future by those funding, organising and attending conferences remains to be seen. What we do know, though, is that, while conferencing is such an integral—if somewhat bizarre, often misunderstood and sometimes despised— part of academic work and career progression, academics will find ways to conference, no matter what.

6.6 Further resources: Thinking about conferences

Conference inclusivity and belonging:

- Black, A. L., Crimmins, G., Dwyer, R., & Lister, V. (2020). Engendering belonging: Thoughtful gatherings with/in online and virtual spaces. *Gender and Education, 32*(1), 115–129. doi:10.1080/09540253.2019.1680808
- Henderson, E. F., & Burford, J. (2020b). Thoughtful gatherings: Gendering conferences as spaces of learning, knowledge production and community. *Gender and Education, 32*(1), 1–10. doi:10.1080/09540253.2019.1691718
- Rodríguez-Zulaica, A., & Ara, A. F.-V. (2019). Measuring accessibility in MICE venues: The case of the Euskalduna Conference Centre (Bilbao, Spain). In R. Finkel, B. Sharp, & M. Sweeney (Eds.), *Accessibility,*

Inclusion, and Diversity in Critical Event Studies (pp. 209–217). London; New York, NY: Routledge.
- Walkington, H., Hill, J., & Kneale, P. E. (2017). Reciprocal elucidation: A student-led pedagogy in multidisciplinary undergraduate research conferences. *Higher Education Research & Development*, *36*(2), 416–429. doi:10.1080/07294360.2016.1208155
- Walters, T. (2018). Gender equality in academic tourism, hospitality, leisure and events conferences. *Journal of Policy Research in Tourism, Leisure and Events, 10*(1), 17–32. doi:10.1080/19407963.2018.1403165

Democratisation of knowledge production and circulation:

- Koch, S. & Matviichuk, E. (2021). Patterns of inequality in global forest science conferences: An analysis of actors involved in UUFRO world congresses with a focus on gender and geography. *Forest Policy and Economics, 129,* 1–12. Doi: 10.1016/j.forpol.2021.102510
- Niner, H. J., & Wassermann, S. N. (2021). Better for whom? Leveling the Injustices of International Conferences by Moving Online. *Frontiers in Marine Science, 8*(146). doi:10.3389/fmars.2021.638025

Environmental and sustainability concerns:

- Bousema, T., Selvaraj, P., Djimde, A. A., Yakar, D., Hagedorn, B., Pratt, A., Barret, D., Whitfield, K., & Cohen, J. M. (2020). Reducing the carbon footprint of academic conferences: The example of the American Society of Tropical Medicine and Hygiene. *The American Journal of Tropical Medicine and Hygiene, 103*(5), 1758–1761. Doi: 10.4269/ajtmh.20–1013

- Chalvatzis, K., & Ormosi, P.L. 2020. The carbon impact of flying to economics conferences: Is flying more associated with more citations? *Journal of Sustainable Tourism, 29*(1), 40–67. Doi: 10.1080/09669582.2020.1806858

The fragility and resilience of conferences:

- Donlon, E. (2021). Lost and found: The academic conference in pandemic and post-pandemic times, *Irish Educational Studies, 40*(2), 367–373 DOI: 10.1080/03323315.2021.1932554
- Reinhard, D., Stafford, M.C., & Payne, T.C. (2021). COVID-19 and academia: Considering the future of academic conferencing. *Journal of Criminal Justice Education, 32*(2), 171–185. doi: 10.1080/10511253.2020.1871047

References

Ahmed, S. (2012). *On being included: Racism and diversity in institutional life*. Durham, NC: Duke University Press.

Alananzeh, O., Maaiah, B., Al-Badarneh, M., & Al-Shorman, A. (2017). The geographic distribution of conferences in Jordan from 2014 to 2016 using predictive GIS modeling. *Journal of Convention & Event Tourism*, 1–19. doi:10.1080/15470148.2017.1406832

Barron, R. J. (2020). Interrupting conferences: Sex workers and public protest. *Gender and Education, 32*(1), 130–136. doi:10.1080/09540253.2019.1633463

Basch, F. (2001). Moulin d'Andé, France 1978–1979, Shaker Mill Farm, USA 1982. *Cahiers du CEDREF*, 37–40.

Black, A. L., Crimmins, G., Dwyer, R., & Lister, V. (2020). Engendering belonging: Thoughtful gatherings with/in online and virtual spaces. *Gender and Education, 32*(1), 115–129. doi:10.1080/09540253.2019.1680808

Boger, C. A., Varghese, N., & Rittapirom, S. D. (2005). The impact of the September 11 attacks on airline arrivals and conventions in nine major U.S. cities. *Journal of Convention & Event Tourism, 7*(2), 21–41. doi:10.1300/J452v07n02_02

Bousema, T., Selvaraj, P., Djimde, A. A., Yakar, D., Hagedorn, B., Pratt, A., Barret, D., Whitfield, K., & Cohen, J. M. (2020). Reducing the carbon footprint of academic conferences: The example of the American Society of Tropical Medicine and Hygiene. *The American Journal of Tropical Medicine and Hygiene, 103*(5), 1758–1761. doi:10.4269/ajtmh.20-1013

Campos, R., Leon, F., & McQuillin, B. (2018). Lost in the storm: The academic collaborations that went missing in Hurricane Issac. *The Economic Journal, 128*(610), 995–1018. doi:10.1111/ecoj.12566

Carpay, J. (2001). A conference that couldn't take place. *Mind, Culture, and Activity, 8*(3), 268–271. doi:10.1207/s15327884mca0803_5

Chalvatzis, K., & Ormosi, P.L. (2020). The carbon impact of flying to economics conferences: Is flying more associated with more citations? *Journal of Sustainable Tourism, 29*(1), 40–67. doi:10.1080/09669582.2020.1806858

Connell, R. (2017). Southern theory and world universities. *Higher Education Research & Development, 36*(1), 4–15, doi:10.1080/07294360.2017.1252311

Dawson, M. (2020). Rehumanising the university for an alternative future: Decolonisation, alternative epistemologies and cognitive justice. *Identities, 27*(1), 71–90. doi:10.1080/1070289X.2019.1611072

Derudder, B., & Liu, X. (2016). How international is the Annual Meeting of the Association of American Geographers? A social network analysis perspective. *Environment and Planning A, 48*(2), 309–329. doi:10.1177/0308518x15611892

Donlon, E. (2021). Lost and found: The academic conference in pandemic and post-pandemic times. *Irish Educational Studies, 40*(2), 367–373 doi:10.1080/03323315.2021.1932554

Dubrow, J. K., Kołczyńska, M., Slomczynski, K. M., & Tomescu-Dubrow, I. (2015). Sociologists everywhere: Country representation in conferences hosted by the International Sociological Association, 1990–2012. *Current Sociology, 66*(3), 466–489. doi:10.1177/0011392115590612

Elliott, A., & Urry, J. (2010). *Mobile lives*. London; New York, NY: Routledge.

Henderson, E. F., & Burford, J. (2020b). Thoughtful gatherings: Gendering conferences as spaces of learning, knowledge production and community. *Gender and Education, 32*(1), 1–10. doi:10.1080/09540253.2019.1691718

King, J. (2019, 17 December). Multiplying connections, cutting carbon: An experiment in multi-site, digitally linked, flightless conferencing. [Blog post]. *Conference Inference: Blogging the World of Conferences*. Available: https://conferenceinference.wordpress.com/2019/12/17/multiplying-connections-cutting-carbon-an-experiment-in-multi-site-digitally-linked-flightless-conferencing-joshua-king/ (25 January 2022).

Koch, S. & Matviichuk, E. (2021). Patterns of inequality in global forest science conferences: An analysis of actors involved in UUFRO world congresses with a focus on gender and geography. *Forest Policy and Economics, 129*, 1–12. doi:10.1016/j.forpol.2021.102510

Krishna, S. (2007). Feminist perspectives and the struggle to transform the disciplines: Report of the IAWS southern regional workshop. *Indian Journal of Gender Studies, 14*(3), 499–515. doi:10.1177/097152150701400307

Mair, J. (2014). *Conferences and conventions: A research perspective*. London; New York, NY: Routledge.

Manathunga, C. (2018). Decolonising the curriculum: Southern interrogations of time, place and knowledge. *Scholarship of Teaching and Learning in the South, 2*(1), 95–111. doi:10.36615/sotls.v2i1.23

Nshemereirwe, C. (2018). Tear down visa barriers that block scholarship. *Nature, 563*(7729), 7. doi:10.1038/d41586-018-07179-2.

Reinhard, D., Stafford, M. C., & Payne, T. C. (2021). COVID-19 and academia: Considering the future of academic conferencing. *Journal of Criminal Justice Education*, 32(2), 171–185. doi:10.1080/10511253.2020.1871047

Rodríguez-Zulaica, A., & Ara, A. F.-V. (2019). Measuring accessibility in MICE venues: The case of the Euskalduna Conference Centre (Bilbao, Spain). In R. Finkel, B. Sharp, & M. Sweeney (Eds.), *Accessibility, Inclusion, and Diversity in Critical Event Studies* (pp. 209–217). London; New York, NY: Routledge

van Ewijk, S. & Hoekman, P. (2021). Emission reduction potentials for academic conference travel. *Journal of Industrial Ecology, 25*, 778–788. https://doi.org/10.1111/jiec.13079

Walkington, H., Hill, J., & Kneale, P. E. (2017). Reciprocal elucidation: A student-led pedagogy in multidisciplinary undergraduate research conferences. *Higher Education Research & Development*, *36*(2), 416–429. doi:10.1080/07294360.2016.1208155

Walters, T. (2018). Gender equality in academic tourism, hospitality, leisure and events conferences. *Journal of Policy Research in Tourism, Leisure and Events, 10*(1), 17–32. doi:10.1080/19407963.2018.1403165

7 Conclusion

In this book, we have sketched out some of the key elements frequently involved in academic conferencing, unpacking the opportunities these events offer for individual scholars, research fields, and the wider communities we serve. We wrote this book because we know that conferences can be bewildering events for new entrants to the world of research. As the authors of this book, our goal has been to illuminate what happens at conferences, shining a light on aspects that appear particularly perplexing or issues that we feel would benefit from deeper consideration. We have taken a particular focus on how researchers might select and then prepare for a conference, as this is key information that early career researchers are often missing. We have also focused on 'being there' and participating in conferences, because this element of conference practice is often overshadowed by other elements in existing advice literature and professional development workshops. In addition to introducing some of these fundamental aspects of conferencing, we have also sought to help readers *make sense of conferences* on a deeper level—we hope we have persuaded you of the value of reflecting on the process of travelling to a conference, or being an audience member, presenter, organiser, and thinker in relation to such gatherings.

While we hope that this book has offered some useful maps for researchers to call upon, it is important to remember that no researcher can rely on maps alone. It is important to test out the material we have shared in this book in your own context—for example, your particular research field or national location. As we have demonstrated across this book, a 'conference' is not a universal kind of event that plays out in exactly the same way across different contexts. It is inevitably grounded in local ways of gathering, and discipline-inflected ideas of how to communicate knowledge, which means that each conference has its own rituals and customs that might be adhered to. We would encourage you to discuss some of the ideas you have learned from this book with your disciplinary peers and academic supervisors, *and* to talk to your friends and colleagues in other fields too to find out how they 'do' conferences. This can be a wonderful way to cross-fertilise across disciplinary silos. Perhaps there are things you can learn from talking to others outside of your discipline that might inspire you to approach conferences differently in the future.

A key objective we have had in this book is to strike a balance between 'decoding' conferences (i.e., explaining some of the often tacit things that tend to happen at them) and 'thinking about' conferences (i.e., questioning whether the things that tend to happen at conferences are right, and whether they could be improved or done differently). After reading these chapters you might have formed a sense about what we think, and how we like to be at conferences. Some of the values that underpin our thinking about conferences mean that we see them as spaces of care, nurture, and development for researchers and scholarly communities, as well as zones for the robust discussion of academic knowledge. We also see

Conclusion 175

them as sites where harmful norms that structure the academic profession tend to be reproduced, but that there are also opportunities for these norms to be identified and subverted too.

Some readers may have hoped that this book would have served as more of a directive guide than it is. We have tried our best to resist the urge to do too much of this 'directing'—but for a good reason! We don't believe that it helps anyone for us to pretend that conferences are actually really simple and all you need to do is 1–2–3. We don't think that telling you how to be, or pretending that there is even one good way to be at a conference, is a good idea. The thing to do is not to merely follow a list of instructions, but to think about who you are and who you want to be for yourself, and the community of scholars you are a part of. Rather than come to this book project with a sense we would be able to tell you what to do or how to think, we have hoped to open up conferences as an interesting area to become curious about. You may have come to the book because you are presenting or organising a conference, and we hope you may come away from it thinking about other aspects of conferences. Perhaps you came to this book because you find conferences very challenging—both accessing them and being at them. Sadly, this is not a problem we can resolve. But we can reassure you that many people, even the two of us sometimes, feel similarly.

In writing this book, we have had countless conversations with each other and with others about what we think conferences are, what we think they currently do and perhaps should do in the future, and how we want to communicate about them to others. Given that we have a long-term fascination with this strange phenomenon, we hope we have shared some of this passion with you. We have found that the more you look around for conferences, the more you see. Emily has even been a part of a project which has found them all over novels, movies, TV shows, and the like (Reynolds & Henderson, 2022; Henderson & Reynolds, 2022. There wouldn't be this book about conferences without the conference which led us to meet, become friends, collaborators, colleagues, and co-authors. Perhaps you are keen to turn up with your eyes open to all the new and interesting things that might be happening there, all of the subtle social dynamics, all of the moments where *something* seems to happen, and you feel like you are really witnessing live knowledge production in action. Conferences can be banal, boring, run-of-the-mill, but there is always the possibility that a new field might be founded, a key insight might accumulate, you might meet the love of your life or a potential supervisor or post-doc mentor. A key invitation that we have threaded through this book is this: think about *who you are* and *who you want to be* at conferences. While conferences—with all their formality, norms, and conventions—can constrain the selves we bring forward, they can also offer radical opportunities for experimentation and play. We hope this book has offered you possibilities—ways you might think of yourself in relation to conferences.

It's a popular thing for academics to say 'no more conferences!'—and strangely enough, even though we are conference studies researchers, we have some sympathy for this sentiment! Conferences have plenty of ethical problems—which academic communities need to take seriously. But ignoring conferences isn't an option; academic gatherings are here to stay because they enable researchers to exchange knowledge and build relationships that sustain the research endeavour. Thus, we conclude this book with the firm belief that academic conferences have a future. It's now over to you—and all of us who work in and around universities—to shape what the future of these events will look like.

References

Henderson, E. F. & Reynolds, P. J. (2022). 'Mobile, hierarchical, decadent and conflict prone: understanding academia through fictional conferences. *Higher Education.* doi:10.1007/s10734-022-00885-x

Reynolds, P. J. & Henderson, E. F. (2022). Gender and the symbolic power of academic conferences in fictional texts. *Higher Education Research and Development.* doi:10.1080/07294360.2022.2089097

Index

Note: *Italic* page numbers refer to figures.

abstracts: crafting of 80, 82, 83, 89–90, 103; preparation of 79–83
academic career development 7
academic conference industry 132, 160
academic conferences 26; academic associations 5; annual meeting 4; curiosity with 7–11; definition 2–5; digital poster sessions 4; face-to-face conferences 12; income for convention centres 166; key gathering points 5; keynote 4; online conferences 12; organising of 108
ad hoc conference 116–117
American Educational Research Association (AERA) 4
annual conferences 8, 24
asking questions 51–57, 147
athletic conference 2
attending conferences 7, 35, 128, 164, 168

audiences 4–6, 12–16, 49–63, 80, 82, 86–88, 91, 93, 95–99, 101, 104, 128, 135, 137, 138, 154, 159, 173

backup plan 96
Barron, R. J. 158
belonging agenda, for conferences 147–155
blogging 73
'boutique' conference 4, 26
boycotting strategy 29, 30, 150, 165
Burford, J. 8–10, 25, 31, 38, 39, 48, 70, 125
bursaries 31, 35, 134, 138, 155

calls for conference papers (CFP) 8, 23
calls for papers (CFP) 8, 23, 81, 86, 89, 157–158
care responsibilities 9, 14, 35, 36, 43
chat windows 59, 96, 101, 154
citation politics 54

clothing 14, 39, 40, 152
conference: academic knowledge 174; discipline-inflected ideas 174; discussion 63–66; ethical problems 176; Eve Tuck's process 63; fundamental aspects 173; introducing colleagues 59–60; lunchtime presentation 73; Q&A session 51–57; session chair/moderator 57–63; timekeeper 60; welcome and gathering 60
conference abstract 10, 15, 34, 80–83, 129
conference aims 110, 112–114
conference baggage *19*
conference belonging 147–155
conference booklet 14, 46–51, 67
conference cancellation 165, 166
conference chair/conference leadership 26, 58, 119–123
conference committee 151–152
conference curriculum 148, 157, 165
conference delegates 4, 7, 24, 37, 47, 152, 163
conference design 15, 111–114, 127; ad hoc conference 116–117; pre-promised conference 114–115; regular conference 113–114
conference disco 14, 33, 72
conference embodiment 69, 70
conference ethos 15
conference evaluation 15, 140–142
conference food/meals 32, 33, 69–72
conference fragility 164–168
conference funding 26, 30–33, 79, 87, 126, 134
conference inclusivity 147–156
conference inference blog 9, 64, 70
conference leadership 123
conference location 7, 24, 27, 28, 47, 78, 79, 97, 102, 157, 165, 174
conference networking 66–69; hashtag 68; online events 66; poster sessions 68; pre-planning 67; social media accounts 67; website 67
conference organising 153, 164, 165
conference organising team 47, 108
conference papers (CFP) 23, 64
conference pedagogies 86, 103, 124, 125
conference planning 20, 22
conference presenting *78*, 78–79; abstract preparation 79–83; choosing a presentation type 83–89; post-presentation period 100–104; presentation preparation 89–93; Q&A session 98–100; technology and social media 93–97

conference programme 39, 46, 50, 81, 85
conference purpose 111, 112, 127–129, 132
conference registration 136, 137
conference resilience 16, 147, 164–168
conference safety 14, 28, 38
conference selection 24, 43, 80, 131
conference technology 93–97
conference travel 13, 14, 19–43, 160, 162, 167, 168; carbon footprint of 160, 161
conference websites 26, 46–48, 81, 102, 152
Connell, R. 51, 53, 54, 92
countless conversations 68, 175
COVID-19 pandemic 21, 24, 115, 125, 126, 136, 138, 160, 165–168; conference cancellation 165, 166; impact on conferencing 160, 165–168
crafting, abstract 80, 82, 83, 89–90, 103
critical conference studies 176
critical pedagogy 125
Critical Race and Indigenous Studies 62

decoding conferences 12, 174
delegates of colour 92, 152
democratisation, of knowledge production and circulation 156–159

democratising knowledge production 97, 159
'desk reject' 80
digital academic identity 23, 34
digital poster sessions 4
discipline conferences 23, 25
discussants/respondants 63–66, 87
diversity decisions 155, 165
doctoral students 25, 109, 114, 116, 158

environmental concerns, thoughtful conferencing 159–164
environment and sustainability 159–164
equity, diversity and inclusion (EDI) 15, 16
event organisation 108, 109
events industry 109, 162, 166

Facebook 23
face-to-face conferences 12, 60
face-to-face poster presentation 90
feedback 6, 83, 88, 102
feminist pedagogy 124
food and accommodation 136, 137
fragility, of conferences 164–168
friendship 8, 11, 72, 117, 118, 124
funding schemes 30, 134

gender 10, 25, 54, 60, 153
gender policing 151–154
global conference industry 16, 159–160

Global North 29, 89, 132, 133, 156
Global South 29, 133
good conference citizens 153–154
'good' guests 41, 42
graphic recording 130
green conferences 162

hashtag 34, 68
Henderson, E. F. 8–10, 31, 48, 101, 103, 114, 131, 135, 158, 176
honorarium 129
hosting 102, 117, 136, 140, 151
hybrid conference 125–126

inclusivity agenda, for conferences 147–155
Indigenous communities 41, 60, 133, 153
in/equality axes, conferences 149, 150
in-person conferences 20, 32, 36, 42, 70, 100, 126, 135, 136, 140, 160–162, 166
International Academic Identities Conference 70
international conferences 113, 157, 159
Introduction, Methods, Results, Discussion, and Conclusion (IMRAD) 92

keynote 3–4, 26, 27, 67, 68, 102, 113, 129, 130, 139, 164
keynote speakers 157, 164
Khoo, T. 63

knowledge production and circulation, democratisation of 97, 148, 151, 156–159

LGBTQ+ delegates 153
LinkedIn 23, 34, 72
livetweeting 97
local conferences 161, 162

Mair, J. 166
manel(s) 29, 150
McCrostie, J. 28
mega-conference 26
'more of a comment than a question' 56
multi-site conferences 161

National Women's Studies Association 135
neo-colonial forces 156
networking 13, 14, 22, 33, 34, 49, 66–70, 72, 84, 125, 126, 131, 160
Nichols, Rhiannon *78*, *146*
no-platforming 150–151

online chairing 59
online conferences 12, 26, 29, 59, 60, 62, 101, 125, 126, 131, 134, 139, 154, 157–158, 160–161, 164, 166–167
online presentations 96, 101
oral presentation 83–86, 88, 90
organising conferences 5, 13, 15, 58, 107–142; academic associations and learned societies 107; aligning conference design 111–113;

components 126–131; conference evaluation 140–142; food and accommodation 136; half-day event 133; one-day event 116; online and hybrid modes 125; pedagogical approaches 124–126; practicalities 132–140; promotion criteria 108; purpose and aims 110–111; registration desk *107*; research project proposal 107–108; risk management and contingency planning 138; roles and approaches 117–124; universal template 110; without reference 109; work-life balance 118

parent-teacher conference 2
peer review 27, 79, 83, 85, 129
peripheral destinations 132–133
plenary sessions 3, 130
plenary speakers 139, 151
post-conference actions 72–74
poster presentation 84–85, 88, 90
poster sessions 4, 68, 84
post-presentation period, conference presenting 100–104
PowerPoint 91, 94, 95
pre-conference: challenges 22; funding support 30–33; information 22; inter-/trans-disciplinary 21; key consideration 36–43; learning about 20–23; planning 20; preparation 33–36; selection 23–30; steps 19–20
predatory conferences 14, 27–28
pre-planning 67
pre-promised conference 114–115
presentation, conference presenting: preparation of 89–93; type 83–89
presenting at conferences *78*, 78–79; abstract preparation 79–83; choosing a presentation type 83–89; oral presentation conference posters 83, 90; post-presentation period 100–104; presentation preparation 89–93; Q&A session 98–100; technology and social media 93–97
press conference 2
Prezi programme 95
pronouns 60

question and answer (Q&A) session 15, 51–57, 62, 63, 79, 98–100

racial discrimination 29
regular conference 113–114
ResearchGate 34, 102
resilience, of conferences 164–168
round table 4, 79, 84, 86–90, 128, 151

'safer' presentation mode 88, 89, 99
self-funding 32, 133, 156
seminars 3
session chair 10, 14, 57, 58, 60, 63
sexual harassment 29, 152
sign-language 152, 155
slides 93–95
social media 67, 72, 73, 79, 93–97, 101, 102, 141, 154, 160, 165; in conference presenting 93–97, 102
speaker choice 150, 151
special interest groups (SIGs) 3
subversion 89
supervisors 13, 22, 24, 27, 31, 32, 37, 49, 73, 85, 103, 176
sustainability concerns, thoughtful conferencing 159–164
symposium 3, 8, 64, 84, 86–90, 128, 151

technology 15, 20, 21, 59, 93–97, 103, 104, 165; in conference presenting 93–97

thoughtful conferencing *146*, 146–147; environmental and sustainability concerns 159–164; fragility and resilience 164–168; inclusivity and belonging 147–155; knowledge production and circulation 156–159
traditional conference 114, 129
Tuck, E. 63
Twitter 23, 34, 63, 67, 72, 97

unconferences 125
undeniably conferences 156

visas 37, 156, 164

websites 67, 141
welcome and gathering 41, 60, 133
whanels/wanels 29, 150
women delegates 35, 97, 153
Women's and Gender Studies conferences 124
work-life balance 118
workshop 4, 10, 32, 47, 79, 84–90, 117, 159, 173